P9-AOV-736

3 2911 03225759 4

KF
9223
.5
Z18
1966

FREE PRESS, FAIR TRIAL

FREE PRESS.
FAIR TRIAL

FREE PRESS, FAIR TRIAL

by Sidney Zagri

CHAS. HALLBERG & COMPANY
Publishers
CHICAGO, ILLINOIS 60610

© 1966 by James Clay. All rights reserved.
No part of this book may be reproduced without
permission in writing from the publisher.
Manufactured in the United States of America.
First printing, September, 1966.

Library of Congress Catalog Card Number: 66-27490

KF
9223
.5
.Z18
1966

Contents

Gl28Ag67

212791

J0

Sidney Zagri is a Civil Libertarian. And he considers that so-
briquet the very highest honor and acknowledges
it with dignity and pride.

A native Californian, Zagri graduated from
UCLA in 1935. He attended Harvard Law School
for two years (until the Depression caught up
with him), dropped out to work and save money,
then took his LL.B at the University of Wisconsin.

After law school, Zagri worked for the National Labor Relations Board as an assistant to
the Chief Trial Examiner and later as an impartial chairman in the Labor Dispute Section of
the National War Labor Board. In 1945 he returned to California and entered private practice.
Soon he was deeply involved in the quasi-political
affairs of several citizens' action committees. In
time he combined his two main interests—labor
unions and public affairs—by accepting the job
of directing the community action program for
a large Teamsters' Local in St. Louis.

The road led to Washington and the responsibility of serving the 1,700,000-member International Brotherhood of Teamsters as Legislative
Counsel. It is in this capacity that Sidney Zagri
has attracted worldwide attention as an out-
standing and expert advocate of civil liberties,
not just for Teamsters, but for free men every-
where. He has lectured at major colleges and
universities including the University of Chicago,
George Washington University, the London School
of Economics, and Kings College, Cambridge.

Introduction

The efforts of Mr. Sidney Zagri to effect national legislation to cure some of the evils of trial by newspaper represents something of a switch in the area of the legislative process. Legislative counsel are generally engaged in the business of furthuring the private interests of their clients. After all, that is what they are paid for. And a large part of Mr. Zagri's job is doing just that. But Zagri and his employers have often taken a different view of his role. They frequently assume that what is good for the country may also be good for the union that Mr. Zagri represents. And the actions by Mr. Zagri culminating in this volume are evidence of that evaluation.

I don't mean to suggest that Mr. Zagri's fight for legislation aimed at curbing the abuses that result from using the public press to influence judicial tribunals was totally disinterested. Certainly the Teamsters — and Mr. Hoffa — learned of the problem the hard way, as Mr. Zagri's essay reveals. On the other hand, it should be noted that any legislation that might result would hardly be efficacious in curing whatever injuries had been imposed in the past by the derelictions of the Department of Justice in dealing with the Teamsters and Mr. Hoffa. It is rare that a litigant who has suffered abuses that might be prevented by legislation takes up the cudgels on behalf of such legislation. Legislation is ordinarily prospective in its effect and, therefore, of little benefit or interest to those who have already been imposed upon. It is for this reason that the activities of Mr. Zagri on behalf of the legislation he sponsors herein is extraordinary.

The problem of trial by newspaper has bothered the American bar and judiciary for a very long time. It has been assumed that the very efficacious sanctions that the English use to assure an untainted trial to defendants in criminal cases are unavailable to American courts because of the restraints of the First Amendment. The judicial process has worked out an unsatisfactory solution: leaving the newspapers — and in this day television and magazine publication are implicitly included in that term — to publish what they will, but affording new trials in the more blatant cases of press interference in the administration of the criminal law. The bar associations seem to have put their faith in unenforcible codes of ethics to inhibit the misbehavior of the bar. The legislatures throughout the country have remained silent. Trial by newspaper is an acknowledged evil about which everyone has talked; but no one has done anything about it.

The failure of legislation is explicable. Two of the strongest political forces in the country op- pose interference in anyway with this primitive form of trial by the ordeal of publicity. The news- papers and the public prosecutors have been, as they still are, almost uniformly lined up in op- position to any legislation that threatens in any way to limit the abuses committed by them. It would take a strong-minded legislature to buck these forces. And, until Mr. Zagri's efforts, no legislator volunteered for what might be the role of a political martyr. But Mr. Zagri found some of these independent spirits in Senator Wayne Morse and his colleagues who were prepared to sponsor appropriate legislation in this field. And, solely as a result of such courage, some improvements have already taken place.

The bill introduced by Senator Morse was adopted by the Judicial Conference of the United States. The Department of Justice, for the first time, with the threat of legislation upon it, issued a directive to its officials that might — and per- haps has — cut down on some of the blatant mis- behavior in which they have engaged in the past. Committee hearings have been held in the United States Senate before a joint committee presided over by Senators Ervin and Tydings. But the bat- tle is far from won. If the Senate hearings reveal the depth of the problem, by themselves they do not cure its evils. The Department of Justice di- rective provides no penalties for its violations and, moreover, by its terms it affords the Attorney General the opportunity to ignore its restrictions whenever he sees fit to do so. The Judicial Conference endorsement may be a necessary, but it is hardly a sufficient condition for the effectuation of a cure.

Mr. Zagri's essay and the evidence adduced in support of it mark but the beginning not the end of the road. Perhaps the first step has been taken in securing Congressional attention to the problem. The road ahead is still a long one. The forces defending the reprehensible system of trial by newspaper are fighting a war of attrition. They have unmatched resources to put into the contest. Only an aroused public can help justice to prevail. If, as Mr. Justice Holmes once suggested, truth will prevail in the market place of ideas, it still remains necessary to inform the public of that truth. This is the primary function of this small volume.

Philip B. Kurland

Chicago, Illinois
June, 1966

Philip B. Kurland is Professor of Law at the University of Chicago. He is the author of Religion and The Law: Of Church And State And The Supreme Court *and is editor of* The Supreme Court Review.

FREE PRESS, FAIR TRIAL

FREE PRESS,
FAIR TRIAL

CHAPTER 1

Bread and Circuses

Over a decade ago, Judge Simon H. Rifkind, who had been one of the distinguished judges of the U.S. District Court for the Southern District of New York and has since been a leading lawyer in that community, addressed himself to a major problem in the administration of justice in America today in a piece entitled, "When the Press Collides with Justice."[1] He stated, "If one stops to inspect the collision which occasionally occurs between the courts and the press, one discovers that it is a contest, not between right and wrong, but between two rights... It is a contest between hero and hero, not between hero and villain. In such a tragedy, the end is almost disastrous, and in those unfortunate cases where conflict develops between court and press, the result is frequently disastrous to justice itself..."

The case or cases of U.S. vs. Hoffa is just such a contest and such a tragedy. Here we have a case

[1] Journal of American Judicature Society, (Vol. 34, p. 46, 1960).

history — unparalleled in modern times — where the extra-judicial intrusion of special units of the Government and the mass media into the judicial process resulted in an impairment of high ideal-ism which animates it.

The judicial process functions successfully only if the public feels that it grinds out what they can accept without — to use the title of a recent book — *A Sense of Injustice*. As Judge Simon H. Rifkind stated over a decade ago: "Law loses its norma-tive function the minute the public loses faith in the judicial process and feels that it is a mill that grinds out sometimes justice and sometimes in-justice. Then order can be maintained only by the force of tyranny."

The courts and the legal profession take great pains and resort to much ritual to preserve public confidence in the judicial system. The courts seek jurors free from prejudice; after they are impan-eled, jurors are reminded by the judge that they must decide the case solely on the facts openly adduced in court and in arguments openly heard in court. The judge screens the information which is passed to the jury to make certain that nothing enters which can "pollute the stream of informa-tion upon which the jury is to decide the rights of the litigants." The preservation of the indepen-dence of the judiciary where the course of truth goes on quietly and without fan-fare and where utmost precautions are taken to keep all extrane-ous influences from making themselves felt is maintained fairly well in all cases but one — THE CELEBRATED CASE. A leading jurist noted: "As soon as the cause celebre comes in, the judge and lawyers no longer enjoy a monopoly. They have a partner in the enterprise, and that partner is the press."

"The process of erosion begins long before the trial. The area from which the jury panel is to be called is drenched with all kinds of information — some true, some false — all unchecked by the selective processes of the law, all uncleansed of the dross which it is the object of the law of evidence to exclude. By the time the panel is called to the courthouse, its members have been living in a climate surcharged with emotion either favorable or unfavorable to one of the litigants. To exclude from the jury panel all who have read about the case or heard about it over the radio is to reduce the jury to the blind, the deaf and the illiterate. So the jury must be selected from these precharged human vessels."

It is the celebrated case that presents the real difficulty. As Justice Douglas stated in his address at the University of Colorado on May 10, 1960: "One shudders to think what could be the result in trials having a political cast — where the accused is unpopular, where the charge is inflammatory."

The problem of the Hoffa trial is not a new one. Juvenal hit it squarely when he said: "Two things only the people anxiously desired — bread and circuses.". The Romans provided the populace with bread and circuses in the form of "public trials" in the coliseum; Castro afforded the accused public trials in the ball park in Havana; and in Baghdad, the Government gave the mob a circus in the form of a televised trial of some 70 defendants.

The court was the peoples court; the charge was a plot to assassinate Premier Karim el Kassem. The accused were herded handcuffed into a pen ablaze with klieg lights. A hand-picked studio audience jammed the room. The trial began at 7:00 p.m. to accommodate the television audience. The judge and the prosecutor vied for star billing while the studio audience threw the cues, shouted and applauded.

Televising and broadcasting of Congressional hearings has become another form of public trial in which the entire nation sits as a jury. While the people do not render a verdict of guilty or not guilty in so many words, the television jury often condemns the accused. As Justice Douglas stated, "The television trial may produce evidence to convict the witness, and it may saturate the country with prejudices against the accused that a fair trial may be next to impossible."

The impact of televised Senate Committee hearings on millions of viewers compromised Mr. Hoffa's position in the minds of the American people — in the minds of prospective or actual members of Grand Juries or petit juries considering either indictments against Mr. Hoffa or weighing evidence both for and against Mr. Hoffa in current cases.

Never before in the annals of Congressional Hearings has a witness been brought before a Congressional Committee on 48 separate occasions subjecting him to searching interrogations under the glare of TV lights and exposure to millions of TV viewers over a 2-year period.

Never before had there been such a calloused

disregard of the rights of a witness before a Congressional Committee during the period when the witness was also a defendant in two criminal cases and indictments were being considered by one or more of 27 Grand Juries investigating Hoffa during this period.

Never before had a witness been denied a continuance before a Congressional Committee when that witness was also the accused in a criminal case scheduled for hearing in Federal Court the following week.

Never before had a Congressional Committee instructed its staff to support the government against the witness, but instructed the same staff members to plead congressional or executive privilege when the defense counsel sought to establish that members of the staff or executive branch of the government were responsible for inspiring publicity adverse to the interest of the accused in the criminal case.

The inquisitorial device of subjecting Jimmy Hoffa to searching interrogation during this period, without affording him an opportunity to cross examine an accuser or offer evidence in his own support, replaced the assumption of innocent until proven guilty beyond a reasonable doubt by a presumption of guilty.

These tactics shifting the presumption of innocence to that of guilty tended to undermine the basic tenets of American justice, and reinforced the "guilt image" of Mr. Hoffa in the minds of millions of Americans.

Whether or not the McClellan Committee overstepped its Congressional mandate in both its

conduct of the hearings and the involvement of its
staff in extracurricular activities is the question
raised by Paul Jacobs, staff member of the Center
for the Study of Democratic Institutions, in a
special study.[2]

Regarding the conduct of the Committee, he
points out that, "The Committee was not above
also using anti-union employers to discredit the
Teamsters or capitalizing on a witness' recourse
to the fifth amendment on some questions to ask
other unrelated ones knowing that the fifth amendment would be used again in answer. And the committee charged, for example, that a conspiracy
existed between Teamster officials and underworld characters to open Portland, Oregon, for
gambling and prostitution. But when the final
smoke was cleared from this fiery allegation, *the
committee's own star witness had been convicted
while the Teamster official and the mayor, two of
the committee's main targets, had been acquitted.*"[3]

Mr. David Previant, special Labor Counsel to
the International Brotherhood of Teamsters, has
listed the kinds of "guilt" the committee used
against the union: "We had guilt by association,
guilt by marriage, guilt by eating in the same
chop house, guilt by the general counsel's amaze-
ment, guilt by somebody else taking the Fifth
Amendment, guilt by somebody else refusing to
testify. But we think the 'doozer' was the one that
happened when the committee was taking testimony

---

[2] Paul Jacobs, "Extracurricular Activities of the Mc
Clellan Committee," Reprinted from *California Law
Review*, Vol. 51, May 1963, No. 2.

[3] Ibid., p. 297.

concerning a criminal case in which eight defendants were tried for eleven weeks; the jury was out only eight minutes and came in with the verdict of "not guilty." The police detective who helped prepare the case said the prosecution felt it was not a fair trial. The Committee nodded in sympathy and agreement. This is guilt by acquittal."[4]

Regarding the extra-curricular role of the McClellan Committee, Jacobs finds, "There can be no doubt, for example, that Robert Kennedy and the staff of the McClellan Committee played a noninvestigative, extra-curricular role (1) in the fight against Hoffa within the Teamsters Union, and (2) in assisting the anti-Hoffa representatives on the court-appointed board of monitors in their attempt to use the board as a vehicle for ousting Hoffa and in trying to persuade workers to vote against the Teamsters in a labor board election."[5]

He concludes: ". . . it seems clear to me that the McClellan Committee's direct involvement in the *Cunningham vs. English*[6] law suit, and in the ensuing affairs of the board of monitors, went far beyond the committee's specific mandate and the general mandate of congressional committees. The evidence demonstrates to me that the committee and its staff, under Robert Kennedy's direction, trespassed heavily upon the rights of Hoffa and the union."[7]

---

[4]Central Conference of Teamsters, Proceedings, Sept. 28, 1958.

[5]Supra, Paul Jacobs.

[6]English v. Cunningham, 361 U.S. 905, 909-10 (1959).

[7]Supra, Paul Jacobs.

After two years of investigation and hearings
the Committee had successfully projected Hoffa's
image as one of evil strength. Jacob's observation
on this point is significant: "By the time Hoffa
had completed the first of his numerous appearances before the committee, millions of TV
screens and newspaper photos had made him so
notorious that even the crews on the planes he
flew would leave the cockpit to stare at him,
fascinated by the aura of evil strength that had
been projected around him" [8]

---

[8] Ibid.

CHAPTER 2

Pursuit of Hoffa

In September, 1959, after Kennedy had resigned as counsel to the McClellan Committee in order to run his brother's primary campaign, he continued his extra-curricular relationship with the court appointed Board of Monitors established by agreement with Hoffa and the Teamsters Executive Board. As late as 1960 Kennedy took time out from his brother's campaign to meet with the six of the plaintiffs in *Cunningham vs. English* who had dropped Godfrey Schmidt and retained counsel. The purpose of the meeting was to persuade the plaintiffs to return to Schmidt and urge them to accept McShane as a monitor nominee instead of Lawrence Smith.

The meeting in Kennedy's apartment resulted from the Court of Appeals decision reversing the decision of the lower court's dismissal of Monitor Lawrence Smith.

Robert Kennedy's pursuit of Hoffa continued during the course of his brother's campaign for the Presidency.

On November 6, 1960, one month before the indictment of Hoffa in Orlando, at the time the Grand Jury was convened to consider the charges by the Government, Robert Kennedy appeared on "Meet the Press." Q. "Senator Kennedy has been criticized for something he said in one of the debates with reference to Jimmy Hoffa, and that is, he is unhappy because he is still free. I know you directed that investigation and I wonder if you feel the same way about Hoffa?"

Kennedy: "I think it is an extremely dangerous situation at the present time, this man who has a background of corruption and dishonesty, has misused hundreds of thousands of dollars of Union funds, betrayed the Union membership, sold out the membership, put gangsters and racketeers in positions of power, and still heads the Teamsters Union."

The question arises did the General Counsel of the McClellan Committee transfer his extra-curricular activities of the committee to the office of the Attorney General in his pursuit of Hoffa and if so what form did these activities take and what effect did they have in influencing the administration of justice in the Hoffa case.

In 1961, the first official act of the Attorney General was to establish a "get Hoffa squad;" with Walter Sheridan as its chief. In March, 1961, less than two months later, Bobby Kennedy met with the editors of *Life* magazine for the purpose of planting an expose of Hoffa in *Life* magazine to be published at a time to coincide with one of his pending trials.

Positive proof of this is to be found in the now famous *Life* memo, which was originally produced before the Platform Committees of the Republican National Convention and which subsequently was produced by a witness before the Senate Subcommittee investigating "invasion of privacy" and the authenticity of which was verified by Senator Robert Kennedy in testimony before that Committee.

The anatomy of the conspiracy was thoroughly documented by the editors of *Life* magazine in a personal and confidential inter-office memo of March 6, 1961. It is from Hank Suydam, editorial writer, to E. K. Thompson, Managing Editor.

In March, 1961, Attorney General Kennedy called Hank Suydam of the editorial offices of *Life* magazine in Washington, D.C. and asked him to drop everything and come to the office of the Attorney General on a matter of the utmost importance. After taking the greatest precaution to swear Suydam to secrecy, Kennedy confided that he had in his back room a high-ranking Teamster official, a confidant of Hoffa, who had been working directly with Kennedy in secret since 1959.

Kennedy "had suggested to this man that he make his break with Hoffa by an article in *Life* magazine in the form of a personal expose of Hoffa." Suydam was interested and wanted to meet Sam Baron. He swore him to secrecy and, as he states, he finally met Sam Baron after a "cloak-and-dagger shift of scenery involving Kennedy's slipping us out through a back corridor and driving through roundabout routes to the guy's home in Virginia and assigning to me the code name of 'Brown'."

After the interview with Sam Baron, Suydam

recommended the story to his superior even though "the expose is ... pretty undocumentable and therefore probably very libelous." However, he adds, "the personal stuff on how Hoffa behaves sounds pretty good." In effect, Attorney General Kennedy and the Editors of *Life* magazine were saying, "My mind is made up — don't confuse me with facts." This is irresponsible government and irresponsible journalism.

In the covering letter, dated Thursday, it becomes clear that E. K. Thompson, the managing editor, was interested in the story, that Kennedy was delighted that *Life* was sold on his project and suggested that a ghost writer be assigned to write the story for Sam Baron's signature. It is also clear that *Life* magazine did not believe the Baron story since it could not be supported or documented but nevertheless desired to publish it because of the "personal stuff on how Hoffa behaves."

In other words, a magazine with a circulation of approximately 7 million copies a week was prepared to publish a story about an individual who was about to go on trial even though the data concerning that individual was "undocumentable and probably libelous."

The *Life* memo of March 6, 1961, proves beyond a shadow of a doubt that Kennedy not only arranged for the planted story but also personally became involved in all the sordid details leading to the break between Baron and Hoffa. On page 6 of the "personal and confidential" office memorandum, Suydam stated, "later, Baron turned over many things to Kennedy, including documents."

The following events, perfectly timed to influence the outcome of the Nashville case, became the subject of national press, radio, and T.V. "headlines."

1. Sam Baron did break with Hoffa. He provoked a fight with Hoffa in the office of the General President on May 16, 1962. An altercation followed and Baron swore out a warrant for Hoffa's arrest. This made page one headlines in the newspapers and magazines all over the country.

2. On May 17, 1962, the grand jury in Nashville, Tennessee, returned an indictment against Mr. Hoffa.

3. On July 20, 1962, on the eve of the Nashville trial, a 14-page expose of Hoffa by Sam Baron was published in *Life* magazine as per plan.

This was not the first or the last time that Robert Kennedy used *Life* magazine to influence the outcome of the cases against James R. Hoffa. At the conclusion of the McClellan hearings *Life* magazine published a series of three articles in May and June, 1959, containing such malicious distortions of the truth that even the author of the article disassociated his name from the third article of the series.

In the June 1st issue of *Life*, Robert Kennedy wrote a postscript to the series endorsing the article and underscoring its most vicious and malicious conclusions.

CHAPTER 3

The Slick Magazine Jury

On May 15, 1964, during the period the Hoffa jury was being selected in Chicago, *Life* magazine published as its feature story, "Inside Hoffa's Ugly World and the Plot to Kill Robert Kennedy — by the Man Who Got the Teamster Boss." The story was based exclusively on statements of Ed Partin, who had a potential of 211 years of jail sentences facing him when he agreed to cooperate with the government in "getting Jimmy Hoffa" while he was incarcerated in a Baton Rouge, Louisiana, jail. The charge was that Jimmy Hoffa had approached him to plant a plastic bomb at the Kennedy home for the purpose of assassinating the Attorney General. In order to sell Partin's story as believable, *Life* not only distorted the truth regarding this man's criminal background and family relationships, but also placed their professional journalistic reputation on the line in the following statement: "The lie detector test which verified Partin's story about Hoffa was administered by the nation's foremost expert in the field. He is Leonard Harrelson, President of Leonarde Keeler, Inc., pioneer developers of the device and teachers of its techniques."

According to a story in the *St. Louis Post Dispatch*, February 16, 1962, Harrelson admits to a criminal record and to falsifying his professional background.

Cleve Backster, Chairman of the Academy for Scientific Interrogation — an association dedicated to the advancement of the polygraph as a science — completely attacks the honesty of the Harrelson polygraph test of Partin in his annual report of August 19, 1964, at the 16th Annual Seminar of the Academy for Scientific Interrogation.

Mr. Backster's analysis of the polygraph chart contained on Pages 88 and 89 in the May 15 issue of the *Life* magazine is included in Appendix A. He concludes, "Not only is there no justification to come to the answer that was arrived at (as credited by *Life* to Harrelson), but in all probability it should have gone the other way" (indicating that Partin was being deceptive rather than truthful regarding the allegation concerned).

Congressman John Moss of California sought to investigate the accuracy of the FBI polygraph on Partin in this matter but was turned down by FBI Director Hoover on the grounds that the information is unavailable at this time since there is a case pending in the courts.

The Nation, September 7, 1964, in its editorial, "Trial by Press Release," observes that "The *Life* and *Look* articles, which were clearly instigated by the Department of Justice, were attempts to instruct the jury of public opinion to convict

Hoffa regardless of the character of the evidence to be presented against him in the courtroom."

The personal involvement of Robert Kennedy in the invidious practice of "trial by press release" extends to many other publications, radio and TV.

Clark Mollenhoff, Washington correspondent for the *Des Moines Register* and *Look* magazine, an intimate of Robert Kennedy and Walter Sheridan was given the assignment of writing three major pieces on matters which would effect the outcome of each of three indictments against defendant Hoffa — the second indictment in the wiretap case, the jury tampering indictment resulting from the Test Fleet case in Nashville, Tennesee, and the Chicago trial. In each of these three articles Mollenhoff reached approximately 7 million readers in addition to the millions who were exposed to the general conclusions of the articles in the daily press, radio and TV.

The articles dealt with matters which could have only been disclosed from confidential information in Government files or in the files of the Prosecutor or the Grand Juries. All three articles are in the Appendix of this book. Put in the context of the *U.S. vs. Hoffa,* they constitute a shocking erosion of the principle of fair trial.

1. The Second Trial on Wiretapping

In May, 1958, just before the trial began in June 1958, Clark Mollenhoff and David Zingg sought to influence prospective jurors by writing a piece entitled: "Jimmy Hoffa — The Man Who Out-smarted Himself."

Excerpts from the article appear in Appendix B, but suffice it to say at this point that Mollenhoff described Hoffa as a peevish, brutish and ruthless associate of vicious criminals.

Making no bones about the purpose of the article, the *Look* piece contained the following statement:

"This spring, he stands trial for the second time on wiretapping charges."

2. Jury Tampering Trial

In the May 21, 1963, issue of *Look* magazine, Clark Mollenhoff pursued the pattern established in the wiretap case only with greater success in influencing potential jurors in the Chattanooga trial.

With the Nashville indictment handed down, all stops were pulled out and Clark Mollenhoff did his best to pollute the minds of the Nashville jurors when he wrote for *Look* magazine a piece entitled "Jury Tampering in Tennessee." The article was as positive as the title suggests and paraded as Gospel truth all kinds of suspenseful, dramatic allegations that could not have been admitted evidence in a court room. Lest the idle reader should miss the point, the *Look* article had a picture of Judge Miller, looking young and earnest, and this caption "SHOCKED JUDGE. Judge Miller charged that efforts had been made 'almost before my eyes to influence this jury improperly.'"

The message was clear. Any red-blooded American should be happy to have a chance to serve on the jury and convict Hoffa.

It is shocking that a responsible press would discuss specific charges of jury tampering after an indictment had been handed down on this very issue and before the trial. This blatant disregard of the defendant's rights cannot be fully understood unless the article itself is read. (See Appendix C)

3. Chicago Trial

On May 19, 1964, while the jury was being impaneled in the Chicago trial of James R. Hoffa, Clark Mollenhoff once again pursued his favorite pastime — influencing prospective jurors in the cases of *U.S. vs. Hoffa*. This time the topic was "The Plot to Assassinate Robert Kennedy." (Appendix D) It appeared four days after the same subject matter was discussed in the aforementioned article in *Life* magazine. The article did not deal with any details concerning the assassination plot but the sensational and shocking nature of the title had served the purpose of getting the attention of prospective jurors who might be influenced by a rehash of Hoffa's prior conviction in Chattanooga, Tennessee.

In each of the Hoffa cases the Justice Department issued a press release summarizing the essential facts of the indictment, but in each instance the presentation of the facts was slanted from the government's point of view. It was this practice that caused Senator Wayne Morse to introduce a bill (S. 290). Senator Morse states in his Senate speech, June 27, 1963:

"These press releases, according to counsel, have the effect of prejudicing his client because, as Senators will see upon reading them, they dig up old cases, old charges, and old indictments and create the impression that the recent indictment is of an individual who allegedly has a bad previous record."

Senator Morse then obtained permission to have a Justice Department press release, "Summary of Past Criminal Actions Against James R. Hoffa" incorporated into the Congressional Record. (See Appendix E)

The misleading nature of these press releases is illustrated by the five-page press release issued by the Department of Justice on June 4, 1963, regarding Hoffa's indictment in Chicago. The press release charged that Hoffa and seven other men had fraudulently obtained $20,000,000 in 14 loans for themselves and others, also charged a diversion of $1,000,000 from the loans for their personal benefits.

Sensational nature of the release made page one in all Metropolitan papers throughout the country. The *Chicago Daily News* as an example, ran the story on page one and inside. A subhead stated "One Million Dollars 'Diverted' United States Says".

The uninformed public was left with the impression that the Teamsters Pension Fund was $1,000,000 short, but it was not one nickel short. During the trial, the defense offered to prove that the fund was not one nickel short but would be $14,000,000 richer when the loans matured. The Government argued that this was irrevelant under the terms of the indictment. The court so held.

This illustrates the misleading nature of the press release which leaves the impression that the fund had been milked to the tune of $1,000,000.

The charge of $1,000,000 diverted as contained in the press release was interpreted by the *Chicago Daily News* in the form of the following heading "Looting of the Pension Fund Charged."

CHAPTER 4

The TV-Radio Jury

The broadcasting industry has an ever-increasing responsibility in exercising restraint concerning communications on matters which might affect the outcome of a pending case.

In November, 1963, the "Roper Survey of Public Attitudes Towards Television" revealed that 55 per cent of the American people said that they got most of their news from television, while 52 per cent named newspapers as compared to 52 per cent for television and 57 per cent for newspapers two years earlier.

We are in the process of analyzing radio and TV reports at this time. However, for the purposes of this record some of the more important broadcasts directly affecting the rights of the defendant Hoffa in one or more of his cases are highlighted.

The broadcasts break down into three categories:
1. Panel Shows
2. News Broadcasts
3. Editorials

Panel Shows:

Program: All America Wants to Know
Date: December 2, 1962
Station: WTTG-TV and the ABC Network

A letter addressed to James Haggerty, Vice-President of ABC protesting the Network's failure to edit the program "All America Wants to Know" signed by Henry Mayer of the law firm, Mayer, Wiener and Mayer, of New York City delineates the outrage:

"Senator John McClellan, when interviewed by reporters about ten days ago regarding the implications of the current National Labor Relations Board contest between the Communications Workers of America and the Teamsters Union over the Western Electric Installers, took the fair and lawyer-like position that since a criminal trial involving charges against James Hoffa was going on in Tennessee, he would make no comment.

"The judicious senatorial toga was doffed completely, however, on WABC on Sunday and was replaced by a hatchet job on the part of the Senator, replete with the usual name calling and, beyond that, the extreme characterizations of Hoffa as 'a menace to society',

'a threat to our national safety and welfare',
as well as the usual tripe about the Teamsters taking control of the nation through its
power to tie up transportation, etc.

"Coupled with the verbal brickbats was the
visual display of McClellan's new book *Crime
Without Punishment,* with the implicit indication to the watchers that Hoffa should not go
scot-free again—all with the obvious hope, that
if Hoffa's 'jury of his peers' were among the
viewers (and they probably were) the 'crime'
this time would not go 'without punishment'."

Another example of the use of the panel show
can be found in the appearance of Bobby Kennedy
on several Jack Paar shows which was used to
further underscore Bobby Kennedy's message from
The Enemy Within as well as to advertise the
condensation of the book in *Reader's Digest* with
a circulation of 17 million.

Jack Parr invited Bobby Kennedy on his show
in May and June of 1959 as well as in March, 1960.
Appendix H includes excerpts from the Robert
Kennedy appearances which were malicious and
calculated to defame the character of James R.
Hoffa. They were a part of an over-all scheme to
project Hoffa as a power-hungry, dangerous, evil
influence.

On the 26th day of July, 1959, Robert Kennedy
continued his tirade against Mr. Hoffa during his
appearance on "Meet the Press" which was broadcast over NBC. Point 22 of Appendix H contains
excerpts from this underscoring and emphasizes
the conclusions stated on numerous occasions in
the press, on radio and TV.

News Broadcasts:

    Program: News of the World
                Morgan Beatty

    Date: May 18, 1962

    Station: WRC Radio and NBC Network

On this program Morgan Beatty announced the indictment of defendant Hoffa and related it to a long history of what he called ". . . an old Teamster Union trial of arson and bribery in Tennessee . . ." He further related it to the expose of the McClellan racketeering. He also related it to the acquittal of thirteen Teamsters by Judge Ralston Schoolfield of Chattanooga who were accused of Tennessee labor violence.

Here are a few choice excerpts from this broadcast:

"MORGAN BEATTY: The news tonight is an old Teamster Union trial of arson and bribery in Tennessee, a trial reopened tonight in the form of crisp, new, hot indictments against Jimmy Hoffa, the Teamsters' boss.

". . . Young Robert Kennedy was the man who exposed the fireseared Tennessee labor jungles before a Senate Committee in 1957. He was then counsel for the McClellan Racket Committee. Hence, before we get to the new hard typewritten words, wrapped in a blue federal jacket, before that, a flash-back to the late 1940's. Testimony before the Senate Rackets Committee revealed that Teamsters in those days were suspected of ruling the labor roost in Tennessee, "with the help of arsonists and highly placed politicians, who took payoffs.

"One judge, Ralston Schoolfield, of Chattanooga — known as turkeyneck — presided at the acquittal of 13 teamsters accused of Tennessee labor violence. Later, Judge Schoolfield was kicked off the bench by an act of the legislature of his state. The main charge was that he accepted an automobile as a gift from a Chattanooga racketeer; another, that he cussed to beat all get-out on the bench. In any event, Jimmy Hoffa and an associate, the late Bert Brennan, chose Tennessee in 1949 to organize a business deal through a corporation known as Test Fleet.

". . . That brings us to today in Nashville, Tennessee. The old Hoffa enemy, Attorney General Kennedy, announced the indictments. Testimony has been going before a federal grand jury in Nashville since February. This time the charge is sharp, clear, direct — illegal payments by Commercial Carriers between May of 1949 and May of 1958 to Hoffa and Brennan through Test Fleet, amount $1,008,057, and the tie between Hoffa and Commercial Carriers was Teamsters Local 299 in Detroit, Michigan. Commercial Carriers, the charge says, did its business of hiring the labor of Teamsters through Local 299 and Hoffa himself is president of his home-town local. Oh, yes, Commercial Carriers is also under indictment."

The following is a sampling of summaries prepared by Radio Reports, Inc. of news broadcasts over a five-day period in July and August, 1962. These broadcasts are particularly significant as they immediately preceded Hoffa's Nashville trial.

August 1 . News of the World, NBC Network, 7:30 P.M.

> Leon Pearson reports on Federal Grand Jury indicting Miami Bank President... real target is Hoffa . . . 40 of Mr. Hoffa's cronies have been indicted . . . Atty. Gen. Kennedy determined to upset Hoffa dynasty by 1964. (Min. Text)

August 1 . NBC News, 10 P.M.

> Richard Harkness reports on govt's far-flung investigation of Hoffa . . . Kennedy's out to get anybody having anything to do with pension fund. . . President of Miami Bank calls indictment a drummed-up charge. (Minimum Text)

July 25 . . Paul Harvey, ABC Network, 6:00 P.M.

> Says Hoffa refuses to speak about his mobster connections . . . a Teamster spokesman says Hoffa will have a statement in the future. (Brief)

July 26 . . News, 4:30 P.M., WTIC-TV (Hartford, Conn.)

Film clip of Mr. Hoffa replying to charges by Sen. McClellan that he is linked to gamblers. (Min. Text)

July 25 . . News of the World, NBC Network, 7:30 P.M.

Morgan Beatty reports that Sen. McClellan threatens to jail all witnesses who do not cooperate with Congressional Committees, and this contains an implied criticism of the Supreme Court . . . It is clear that Hoffa has permitted his lieutenants to be as crooked as they like . . . McClellan wants Congress to have power of arresting . . . (Min. Text)

July 25 . . Alex Dreier, ABC Network, 6:30 P.M.

Hoffa raked over the coals today as Senate Committee calls him a man who doesn't care if his officials deviate from the straight and narrow. Hoffa had no comment.

CHAPTER 5

Solutions

We hear the solution "change of venue" offered as an alternative to corrective legislation. It was characterized by Judge Rifkind over a decade ago as "unrealistic". "Change in venue," he stated, "was all right in the days of the horse and buggy, but today, in a celebrated case, the newspapers and radio blanket the country and most communities are deluged with information and opinion about the case."

A good example of the ineffectiveness of changes of venue may be found in the transfer of the Hoffa case from Nashville to Chattanooga by Judge Frank Wilson.

In granting the transfer, Judge Wilson stated that in the Nashville area "particularly during the period since November 18, 1963, the date upon which an order was entered setting this case for trial upon January 6, 1964, the publicity has been quite intense. An impartial review of this publicity can only lead to the conclusion that it has been prejudicial to each of the defendants herein with respect to the matters upon which he here stands for trial . . ."

It is true that there was extensive publicity in the Nashville papers from November 30 to December 31, the date of the transfer *(Ibid)*. But a review of the Chattanooga publicity shows that substantially the same stories were carried in the Chattanooga papers.

On November 21, 1963, both Chattanooga papers carried a front-page story with respect to Osborn's being disbarred. The *Times* also had a picture of appellant Hoffa with Osborn on the front page. The stories repeated the Nashville charges and stated that Osborn has attempted to contact other jurors in the 1962 Nashville trial. On that day or the following day, both papers published opprobrious editorials, one stating that there had been fixing in Nashville and elsewhere in the Hoffa trials and directed interest and attention to the approaching trial. On November 22, the Osborn story was repeated on the front page of the *Times*. On November 23, the *Times* carried a story on the impending grand jury probe of the Osborn matter, adding that Osborn had used the same middle man, Officer Vick, in an attempted juror fix in Hoffa's 1962 Nashville trial, and that Vick was in hiding under heavy guard of Marshals. Additional prominent stories were carried about the Osborn grand jury probe on November 27 and 28, and December 2, 3, 4, 5 and 6, stating that it was being broadened to others. The December 4, story in the *News Free Press* was on the front page, stating that the Foreman of the 1962 jury had been called before the Grand Jury. The stories stated that the grand jury was under heavy guard. All of these stories associated Osborn with Hoffa and the approaching trial. The *Times* had a front page story on December 6, referring to the many Hoffa trials and the approaching one.

On December 7, when Osborn was indicted, the *News Free Press* carried a front page story that Osborn was indicted on three counts, two for jury tampering in the 1962 trial, bringing the total to 12, including Hoffa, indicted for jury tampering in that trial. These were also front page stories and an editorial about the disbarment of Attorney Beard on December 19. The stories continued almost daily right up to trial time.

The English have a solution. Lord Devlin has described the governing rule in England in his book *The Criminal Prosecution in England* (1953), pp. 119-21:

"This process, for contempt of court, is the weapon used by the court to restrain press comment before and during the trial. It is used in a manner which I am sure would startle some (newspapermen) in the United States. What is sometimes called 'trial by newspaper' is not tolerated in any form."

The English law makes any comment on any matter that is not a part of the evidence that might influence a jury one way or another a basis for contempt of court, even though such comment was innocently done or by an error of judgment or under an honest mistake.

The American law on the subject of contempt as applied to news media is diametrically opposed to the English solution. The Supreme Court has ruled that the utilization of the contempt power to punish publication about any matter that was the subject of litigation is in violation of the provisions of the First Amendment guaranteeing freedom of the press.

> See *Wood v. Georgin,* 370 U. S. (1962): *Craig v. Harney,* 331 U. S. 367 (1947): *Pennekamp v. Florida,* 328 U. S. 331 (1946): *Bridges v. California,* 314 U. S. 252 (1941)

New Trial As the Appropriate Remedy

There is very little doubt that the courts have the power to order a new trial based upon evidence that a jury has been corrupted by newspaper accounts relating to the trial. In *Marshall v. United States* (360 U. S. 310 (1959), the Supreme Court reversed two lower courts that had refused such relief. In *Janko v. United States* (366 U. S. 716 (1961), the court reversed the conviction in which prejudicial newspaper intrusion had poisoned the outcome.

This rule is severely limited by two devices:

1. Leaving the resolution of the question of improper intrusion by the newspaper media of the judicial process to the discretion of the trial court judge, which means, in effect, permitting tainted convictions to stand.

2. Similarly, the rule is often vitiated by the proposition that the burden of showing prejudice is on the defendant, a burden often impossible to establish.

Professor Philip Kurland of the University of Chicago Law School has proposed a statute which would make meaningful the standard of the code in Marshall, Janko, supra. by requiring the defendant to show only that the jury had access to the evidence that would have been excluded from the trial because of its prejudicial nature.

The burden would then shift to the prosecution to show that it had no adverse affect on the conduct of the trial. This solution is to be commended for its simplicity and practicality in application.

Contempt Powers as Applied to
Litigants and Counsel

Senator Morse's bill, S. 290, imposes effective legal sanctions and implements the principles enumerated by the American Bar Association in Canon 20 of the *Code of Ethics:*

> "Newspaper publications by a lawyer as to pending or anticipated litigation may interfere with a fair trial in the courts and otherwise prejudice the due administration of justice. Generally they are to be condemned. If the extreme circumstances of a particular case justify a statement to the public, it is unprofessional to make it anonymously. An *ex parte* reference to the facts should not go beyond quotation from the records and papers on file in the court; but even in extreme cases it is better to avoid *ex parte* statement."

Unfortunately, there are no teeth in the code of ethics that bar associations are so quick to adopt but promptly ignore. The bar has had ample opportunity to police itself. It has thus far refused to do so.

S. 290 would simply adopt the principle expressed by the court in *Henslee v. U. S.*, (246 Federal 2n. 190 (CA 5th 1957).

In this case there was no showing that the publicity secured affected the jury deliberations or that the action of the prosecuting attorney was wilful, as was clearly held in Malinovich:

> "Where, as here, unwanted publicity resulted from action taken by the Assistant United States Attorney in connection with something entirely apart from the proper conduct of the trial, however innocent he may have been of any wilful purpose to influence the jury, a much higher standard prevails. As said by the Supreme Court in *Berger v. United States*, (290 U. S. 78, 55 S. Ct. 629,633, 74L. Ed. 1314):
>
>> 'The United States Attorney is the representative not of an ordinary party to a controversy, but of a sovereignty whose obligation to government impartially is as compelling as its obligation to govern at all; and whose interest, therefore, in a criminal prosecution is not that it shall win a case, but that justice shall be done. As such, he is in a peculiar and very definite sense the servant of the law, the twofold aim of which is that guilt shall not escape or innocence suffer.'
>
> "Without in any way imputing an improper motive to the prosecuting officer here, we do find

that in the proper conduct of the affairs of his office it should have been apparent that for him to file this motion with the inclusion of the self-serving and irrelevant statements of offenses and çrimes not comprehended in the indictment for which Henslee was on trial might well produce the highly unfortunate publicity that actually resulted. His failure to apprehend the natural result of his act is as damaging to the cause of justice as if he had failed in his duty to act with a scrupulous regard for fairness." ID. at 193

Self-Imposed Controls By The Bar, The Press and The Prosecution

The Bar. It is clear from the foregoing that this approach has failed and Canon 20 of the American Bar on this question has been observed more in the breach than in the observance. Similarly, codes by the broadcasting industry and by the press may work in the ordinary case. But the real problem arises in the celebrated case. There the pressures of competition among various segments of the mass media cause the self-imposed regulations to break down.

The Prosecution. The case history of the Hoffa trials demonstrates the extra-judicial intrusion by the prosecutor and exemplifies the problem wherever a celebrated case carries with it political overtones.

For this reason, the Attorney General's memorandum, with laudable guidelines, must necessarily break down in celebrated cases. It is evident that the Attorney General foresees this possibility and for this reason adopted paragraph 9 which states:

> "If a representative of the Department believes that in the interest of the fair administration of justice and the law enforcement process information beyond these guidelines should be released in a particular case, he shall request the permission of the Attorney General or the Deputy Attorney General to do so."

Immediate enactment of S. 290 is a practical solution to a difficult problem. Action should be taken without delay. Wide-spread civil disobedience reflects disregard for the law. Law loses its normative function the minute the public loses faith in the judicial process. It must not feel that the courts "grind out sometimes justice and sometimes injustice."

Enactment of remedial legislation is an important step in restoring lost public confidence.

EDITOR'S NOTE

The documents appearing in this Appendix are eloquent testimony in support of Mr. Zagri's contention that the Government used the mass media as an instrument in its campaign to "get Hoffa." These inflammatory, misleading news stories, television and radio broadcasts, and magazine articles were planted by the Government before and during each of the Hoffa trials for the sole purpose of influencing the outcome of the cases.

None of the alleged statements of fact could have been admitted as evidence in a court of law. The minds of the jurors were thus brainwashed before factual evidence was presented to them.

Appendix

The entire Appendix of this book is reprinted from hearings before the Subcommittee on Improvements in Judicial Machinery of the Committee on the Judiciary, United States Senate, Eighty-Ninth Congress, First Session, on S. 290 and the relationship between the Constitutional right of a free press and the Constitutional guarantees of an impartial trial.

ACADEMY FOR SCIENTIFIC

INTERROGATION

ANNUAL REPORT

(continued)

LIFE MAGAZINE ARTICLE

I am not pulling punches on this one (Backster holding up May 15, 1964, issue of *Life* magazine). This is a disgrace, the polygraph chart that appeared in *Life* magazine (at this time Backster opened the magazine to p. 38 and 89 covering the polygraph portion of a feature entitled "Inside Hoffa's Savage Kingdom." * — Sub-title on p. 88 — "The Lie Detector Confirms His Story" (referring to Edward Partin's accusation). I was really sick when I saw this. I received a telephone call only

---

*Article includes accusation by Edward G. Partin that James R. Hoffa asked him if he could obtain plastic type high explosive which would be used to bomb Robert Kennedy's home.

41

two days later from a congressional sub-committee
asking "what do you think?" (regarding polygraph
examiner Leonard H. Harrelson's chart inter-
pretation). This is like having a tiger by the tail.
If this man Partin, a year or two years from now,
were to say "oh that was a big hoax — and they
missed me on the polygraphy," we could really be
hurt and hurt badly. This (polygraph chart) shows
no indication whatsoever (in support of that which
was reported — regarding Partins truthfulness)
and this happens to be a technique assembly,
though violations of basic all around technique —
rather than subscribing to it — makes it even
more interpretable because the unreviewed "shock"
type questions here don't do a thing to create a
reaction — as compared to the revelant questions
(located nearby). So he (Harrelson) has more in-
gredients of modern technique whether it was
planned that way, or not. This thing is really a
shame. I have received too few inquires about this,
I received two or three calls by telephone, and two
or three people stopped by my office saying "what
do you think of the (May 15, 1964) *Life* magazine
article", and expressing themselves relating to
the unfounded determination. Every one of you
should have been up in arms the minute this thing
came out. Not only is there no justification to
come to the answer that was arrived at (as credited
by *Life* to Harrelson), but in all probably it
should have gone the other way (indicating that
Partin was being deceptive rather than truthful
regarding the allegation concerned). This is not
good (Backster holding up a photographic en-
largement of the approximately half-scale charts

published in *Life*). You all can notice along here the G.S.R. tracing (Backster pointing to the over-all chart), how over-active it is all the way through. Do you notice one little patch of chart where it (the Galvanic Skin Response tracing) is not over-active — one little patch of chart that embraces two questions — where the G.S.R. tracing is not over-active. In my opinion there has been cranked down (G.S.R. amplification) sensitivity in that area.** I base this on the base level where the G.S.R. tracing is "homing" when using the automatic self-centering circuit as was done here. If you maintain the same amplifier sensitivity the G.S.R. tracing would "home" all the way through on the same base line. In other words, the bottom of the recorded tracing, upon returning from any arouseal stablizes at the same base level all the way through any chart that involves no sensivity change. When you change the sensitivity, the tracing "homes" at a different base-level. Here (pointing to the chart location where questions #7 and #8 were asked) it homes at a different location than it did all the way through here (pointing to the remainder of the chart after question #8). And what are these two questions asked on the test? Question number 7: "Did Hoffa ask you if you could get a plastic bomb?" Question number 8: "Did Hoffa say the

---

**Altering of Galvanic Skin Response sensitivity setting while chart is in progress is strictly forbidden unless the change is clearly indicated by the proper chart marking procedure at the very time (and location) where it occurred.

bomb would be used to bomb Kennedy's home?".
Now this may be examiner reinforcement to avoid
confusion regarding that which he believes sincerely to exist. Although this is bad enough, I would
certainly like to think it was only that. If this is
not the reason there are some very serious implications. Now, do we have a "grievance" committee that is really quick to act on a matter
such as this? We have one in name only. When is
the last time we had a grievance filed? I don't
know. There has been one or two in seventeen
years (that I can remember) maybe more than that,
I don't know. Ralph, you probably know. Have there
been three or four — where is Ralph Scharr? Has
there been very much usage of the grievance committee? Not enough, not nearly enough to discipline
ourselves. If we don't start to discipline ourselves
— we are going to have discipline imposed on us —
in a way that we don't like.

LOOK MAGAZINE, MAY, 1958

The man who outsmarted himself

Jimmy Hoffa, one of America's most powerful labor leaders, is a man haunted by his past and faced with the specter of his future.

By CLARK MOLLENHOFF and DAVID ZINGG Look Staff Writers

James Riddle Hoffa, a chunky, cocksure little Napoleon of a man, at 45 has bullied, brawled and bought his way to the top of the mightiest and richest union in America, the International Brotherhood of Teamsters.

He doesn't know it, but by vaulting to power hand in hand with underworld hoodlums and racketeers, he has sown the seeds of his own destruction.

Here is the record as it was unrolled by the Senate labor rackets committee, headed by Sen. John L. McClellan (Dem., Ark.).

Hoffa's grasp for power started with local hoodlums in Detroit and has spread over the nation. As he used racketeers and reformatory graduates to win power, so have criminals used him to strengthen their grip on unionism and business.

Hoffa stands accused by the committee of having "grossly misused" some $2,400,000 in union funds to promote the business interests of himself, his friends and racketeer associates — and for the attendant high cost of keeping them out of jail.

The result has been to place Hoffa in the position of a man who has consumed a potion of a slow-working but fatal poison. The irony is that, in effect, he administered the poison to himself.

Hoffa sees himself impervious to attack. He is confident his union treasury and his union power can buy or crush anyone who gets in his way. But Hoffa's luck may be about to run out. He faces a Federal indictment; his union affairs are watched by three court-appointed monitors; more Senate committee hearings are imminent. These are direct threats to Hoffa and what the committee calls his "hoodlum empire." He also used criminals to gain power but cannot now abandon them without risk to his own life and position.

In the meantime, he wields power that his coal-prospector father never dreamed of. By consorting with gangsters, racketeers and hoodlums, he has placed in his grasp a strategic union that numbers 1.5 million members and has some $37 million in its treasury. Hoffa today is in a position where he can paralyze much of the trucking that roars over America's vital highway arteries. He is also a man who can paralyze businessmen, politicians and other union leaders with fright.

Hoffa learned young to be tough. According to his ex-convict brother, Bill, "If your mother or your father told you to do something, you did it. And they only told you to do it once. The second time, it meant a swat across the mouth."

A quarter of a century after he started on his one-way drive for power, Hoffa was elected president of the Teamsters. His election last fall was staged at a controlled convention spotted with hoods and racketeers, some of them packing revolvers. It was perhaps the most cynical public display of power ever seen in American labor.

Earlier in the year, Hoffa had appeared before the Senate rackets committee. There, the same brilliant mind that had once astonished a lecture audience at Harvard University "forgot" the details of his take-over of Teamster leadership.

Hoffa's memory was vague as to how he had climbed to power with notorious criminals. Nevertheless, the committee introduced testimony and records showing 1) that his Teamster empire is peopled by scores of hoodlums and ex-cons; 2) that

Teamster officialdom has included criminals who operated nonunion businesses with sweatshop wages at the same time that they were representing their own locals; 3) that Teamster officials had used Teamster picket lines to shake down money for themselves from unorganized businesses; 4) that Teamster bosses, many with criminal records, have taken thousands of dollars from union funds to finance their own businesses; 5) that rank-and-file members who protested were threatened and beaten.

Hoffa stands accused before the committee of spending union funds for spying on a grand jury, for the intimidation of witnesses and for expensive lawyers for hoodlums. (A grand-jury witness whose testimony displeased Hoffa once swore to a Michigan judge that Jimmy snapped, "You -----, I'll have you killed.") Union salaries were paid even to jailed labor racketeers.

Little Jimmy Hoffa couldn't have cared less.

As he climbed to the top of the Teamster hierarchy, Hoffa was able to bring himself to view his opponents as inanimate objects, rather than human beings. And while tightening his grip on his Teamster barony, he has managed to do well for Jimmy Hoffa.

The McClellan committee read into the record information that Hoffa had received well over $100,000 in loans from trucking-company officials, Teamster lieutenants, "friends" and union funds.

Hoffa's wife, said the committee, invested about $2,000 in a company that leased trucks to another company having a contract with Hoffa's Teamsters. In a few years, Mrs. Hoffa's profit was close to

$60,000. Hoffa's Detroit Teamster treasury lent money to a friend who says he then lent it to Hoffa. Hoffa personally lent $2,000 or $2,500 to another friend so the friend could start a local union in Detroit. The loan was paid back in the form of "salary" to Mrs. Hoffa and another woman until the payments amounted to $6,000.

John Cye Cheasty, a former Secret Service agent, swore that Hoffa hired him to spy on the McClellan committee's work. Hoffa's offer, said Cheasty, was $18,000. When Hoffa was tried on these bribery and conspiracy charges, he faced a jury of eight Negroes and four whites. At the trial, former heavyweight boxing champion Joe Louis often appeared in court and displayed a touching camaraderie toward the union leader in the presence of the jury. Hoffa was acquitted.

In the course of protecting his own sharklike ascent to the surface of Teamster power, Jimmy Hoffa has given crooks and ruffians cradle-to-the-grave protection. He has always known where to throw his political money. Teamster money has gone to the campaigns of mayors, sheriffs, judges and governors who, as he has often put it, "are on our side." Hoffa supported the aging David Beck, his predecessor, until the time was ripe to knock him off his throne, although Beck hastened the process through his own cupidity. A growing number of observers believe Jimmy Hoffa will follow the same road to discard that was taken by Beck.

It's not that Hoffa is consciously immoral. He is simply amoral. One day in 1955, talking to a reporter in Washington's Mayflower Hotel, Hoffa said, "Everyone has his price. What's yours?"

One prominent East Coast lawyer, who has observed Hoffa closely, says, "He should have been born 400 years ago, in the days of the Italian cabals." He adds that if Hoffa had had any sense of a public standard of morality, his innate brilliance could have made him a great leader.

As it is, his ambitious drive has brewed the powerful poisons that promise his downfall. He has successfully swiveled out of every major legal charge without serving time in jail. But his continued immunity is threatened by time and the public exposure of his acts:

This spring he stands trial for a second time in New York on wiretapping charges.

The AFL-CIO has expelled the Teamsters until they oust Hoffa.

The driving physical pace Hoffa has set for himself first demonstrated its danger when he recently suffered what was described as a "mild" heart attack in Florida.

A court-appointed group of "monitors" armed with stern powers sit in Hoffa's own luxurious headquarters, watching his every move.

Rank-and-file rebellion within the Teamsters may be encouraged by the court fight that led to the appointment of the monitors. A watchful Senate rackets committee stands ready to pounce again.

Even if Hoffa decides under public pressure to clean himself up, it is doubtful that his hoodlum henchmen in the Teamsters would give up their plunder without a fight.

As the callous labor boss goes his lone and ruthless way, it is becoming clear today that Hoffa is the man who outsmarted himself.

LOOK MAGAZINE, MAY 21, 1964

During a friendly
ride with a neighbor,
a juror was offered
$10,000 in "easy money."
The husband of another
juror was promised help
in getting a promotion.
Here is the startling story

of incidents during the

James R. Hoffa trial, which

caused a judge to denounce

JURY

TAMPERING

IN

TENNESSEE

BY CLARK R. MOLLENHOFF

James C. Tippens, a Nashville insuranceman, looked worried as he stepped into the office of Federal Judge William E. Miller on Wednesday, October 24, 1962.

The previous evening, Tippens had listened closely as Judge Miller warned him and other prospective jurors to avoid any discussion that might prejudice them either for or against James R. Hoffa, international president of the Teamsters Union. Tippens was a likely choice as a member of the jury that would try Hoffa and another Teamster official on the charge of accepting $242,000 from a Detroit trucking firm in violation of the Taft-Hartley Act.

The prospective jurors had been excused for the day, before the selection of the jury was completed. Within two hours after he left the Federal Building in Nashville, Tippens was approached by a neighbor who offered him a ride. Since Tippens regarded the man as a friend, he did not hesitate to accept. He had no reason to believe that the neighbor had any interest in the outcome of the Hoffa trial. The neighbor said that Tippens could pick up $10,000 easily and that the money would be paid to him in $100 bills. Initially, the man did not directly link this offer of "easy money" with the Hoffa case. Tippens asked him the direct question: "You are referring to (my) being a prospective juror in the case?"

The man acknowledged that the offer was connected with the case, and urged Tippens to accept it. Tippens said firmly that he did not want to discuss the matter.

He worried about the conversation all night and was still shaken as he entered the Judge's chambers shortly before 9 the next morning. He had resolved to tell Judge Miller about it, even if this might bring trouble to his friend.

Calm and stern-faced, Judge Miller questioned Tippens briefly about the $10,000 offer. The Judge assured Tippens he had acted properly in reporting the incident and instructed him to say nothing about the affair to anyone until he was questioned by the Federal Bureau of Investigation.

Immediately, Judge Miller summoned Government and defense lawyers to his chambers and told them of the incident. In 27 years as lawyer and judge, he said, this was the first time he had heard of such a bold attempt to corrupt the jury system. Judge Miller carefully avoided any contention that Hoffa or Hoffa's lawyers knew of the contact with Tippens, but explained that the contact made it necessary to release Tippens from jury service.

Chief Prosecutor James Neal then commented that a number of improper and illegal telephone calls had been made to prospective jurors. He was concerned that many of the most responsible people would be eliminated from the jury panel by this tactic. "I am inclined to suggest at this point that the jury be locked up," Neal said. "I realize how onerous that is on everyone."

Z. T. (Tommy) Osborn, Jr., one of Hoffa's defense lawyers, objected: "It is an awful long time, and if there is any way to avoid it, your honor should avoid it." Osborn said the calls to jurors were probably the work of "crackpots and do-gooders."

Prosecutor Charles Shaffer said he did not like to inject an "acrimonious note" at an early stage in the trial, but added, "I have no way of relating this to the defendant Hoffa, but . . . the Government does know, and it is a public record, that jurors have been approached before (in cases) in which he was on trial."

Defense lawyer William F. Bufalino lodged a sharp protest: "That is not so . . . I have been in every one of those cases that you have been referring to. I was in the Washington case, the New York cases, and when Bobby Kennedy makes statements (about approaches to jurors) . . . in his book *The Enemy Within,* (that) does not make it a fact."

The decision on "locking up" the jury was a difficult one. Judge Miller commented that it might mean virtual imprisonment of the jurors and alternates for the six or eight weeks the trial was expected to last. Their radio and television programs would have to be censored, their newspapers clipped of stories dealing with the trial, and communication with their families monitored by representatives of the court.

Judge Miller was gravely concerned over the Tippens incident, but the discussion made it seem that further tampering with the jury was unlikely. It appeared to the Judge that only a fool or someone totally corrupt would attempt to contact the Hoffa jurors in the face of such warnings. The jury would not be locked up, at that time, Judge Miller ruled. He also proposed stiff warnings to the jurors and ordered an immediate FBI investigation of the Tippens incident.

In the next nine weeks, Judge Miller's patience was tested as he fought to maintain the decorum of a Federal court — and to avoid the atmosphere of a circus. The Tippens affair was only the first of many incidents that punctuated the lengthy trial of the tough and aggressive 49-year-old Teamster boss.

From the beginning of the trial, U. S. Attorney General Robert F. Kennedy and Assistant Attorney General Hubert (Jack) Miller were seriously concerned about the possibility of jury tampering.

Reports of the Senate's McClellan Committee had alerted investigators of Hoffa's "hoodlum empire" to evidence of earlier efforts to use the Teamsters Union millions to corrupt or influence local law-enforcement officials, prosecutors, judges and committees of Congress.

Kennedy sent Walter Sheridan, a special assistant, to Nashville, to take charge of preventive action. Sheridan was installed in an office across the corridor from the eighth-floor court, and was to have all of the FBI agents necessary for proper investigations. But even with the full services of the FBI, there were serious restrictions on what could be done. The Government had to operate with extreme propriety; corrupters were under no such restraint. The FBI could not question jurors to determine if they had been contacted before the trial. Merely questioning a prospective juror could be regarded as prejudicial to the rights of Hoffa. Even FBI questioning of close relatives or associates of jurors might be regarded as contaminating a juror. If the FBI received a report of suspicious contact with a juror, the juror could not be questioned until the Government was prepared to accept his dismissal.

Under Sheridan's direction, the FBI started a regular surveillance of Hoffa's closest associates. Hoffa's lawyers charged that several hundred FBI agents had flooded the Nashville area and had tapped their telephones. The presence of Government agents at the Andrew Jackson Hotel made it impossible to have frank discussions at dinner while making trial preparations, the lawyers said.

Chief Prosecutor Neal made a formal denial of the charge that telephones were being tapped. The estimate by Hoffa's attorney of the number of FBI agents in Nashville was excessive, but no precise figure was available.

On the night of Saturday, November 17, a group of FBI agents concentrated on the surveillance of two Nashville Teamster officials, Ewing King and George Broda.

FBI Agent Charles Still was posted near King's home when the Nashville Teamster boss got into his 1960 Thunderbird and drove away. Still followed King south to Martin's Restaurant on Murfreesboro Road. At 7:03 p.m. King met Teamster business agent Broda.

Still noted that King opened the rear trunk of the Thunderbird, took out a package and then entered a store building with Broda. When the two Teamsters emerged 15 minutes later, they switched cars. King drove Broda's blue and white 1959 Ford southeast in the direction of the small town of Woodbury. Still followed Broda, who drove King's Thunderbird and returned to his home. There, Still kept watch until 4:20 a.m.

The FBI avoided direct trailing of jurors, but Agents Francis Norwood and Willis S. Turner were on general patrol in Woodbury, the home of one of the jurors. She was Betty Paschal, attractive 35-year-old wife of a Tennessee highway patrolman. Woodbury, a hilly country town more than 50 miles southeast of Nashville, had a population of about 1,600. The FBI needed only a car or two cruising through town or parked at a key point to detect unusual activity, particularly in the early-morning hours.

A strange meeting

It was 1:07 a.m. on November 18 when the agents noticed Broda's Ford parked at the Paschal home. A man in a highway-patrol uniform was standing in the drizzling rain, leaning against the car and talking to the driver. The agents recognized the uniformed patrolman as James Paschal, husband of the juror.

There was little traffic, and the FBI men, not wanting to be conspicuous drove past the Paschal home. At 1:35 a.m., the agents found that both the 1959 Ford and a highway-patrol car were gone. By 2:12 a.m., the highway-patrol car was back in the Paschal driveway.

Other agents on duty in the area noted that King and Paschal met at a desolate wooded spot known as River Springs, three miles south of Woodbury. Instructions were radioed to Agent Warren L. Walsh to go to the vicinity of Lebanon Pike and Old Lebanon Road and to wait there until he saw Ewing King drive past in the 1959 blue-and-white Ford.

Walsh parked as instructed at 2:20 a.m. and remained there until 4:12 a.m., when the Ford passed him. He caught it in his headlights briefly and identified the driver as King. Walsh followed King to his home at 112 Benson Drive where still another agent, Harry T. Posey, was parked in a manner that prevented King from parking. Posey got out of his car, walked to King's car and excused himself: "Sir I will be out of your way in a moment." At the same time, he was assuring himself that the man in the car was King.

Back in Nashville. Walter Sheridan was elated over the nights work, but the Government still needed more pieces of evidence. Some of the pieces did not slip into place until two weeks later.

On December 6, Prosecutors Neal and Shaffer asked for a secret hearing. When the court had been cleared of all spectators. Neal revealed the barest outline of King's contact with the husband of the juror. "These facts create compelling suspicious circumstances indicating an improper approach," Neal said in asking removal of Juror Paschal.

Daniel Maher, one of Hoffa's lawyers, said Neal's revelations were of little consequence. "All that he (Neal) has said is that a juror's home was visited and a person who has been in the courtroom (King) was observed talking to the spouse of the juror.

"What do you think about the head of the Teamsters Union in Nashville swapping cars with someone else and going to the home of a juror?" Judge Miller asked Maher.

"I think it is a circumstance," Maher replied.

"I think it is a shocking state of affairs," Judge Miller snapped.

U. S. Marshal Elmer Disspayne was instructed to bring King and Paschal to the court. King was taken into custody in the courthouse corridor. He entered the court with Disspayne, surveyed the scene momentarily and took the Fifth Amendment on all questions about the early-morning meeting with Paschal.

Prosecutor Shaffer complained that the Nashville Teamster president took the Fifth Amendment after receiving a five-finger sign flashed to him by Hoffa. Defense lawyer Bufalino loudly denied Shaffer's claim. He declared that the Teamster boss only had his hand on his chin as he had frequently during the trial.

"Take your hands down so there won't be any question at all," Judge Miller said to Hoffa.

Oscar (Mud) Pitts, a Teamsters Union member also took the Fifth Amendment when questioned on reports that he had put King in touch with Paschal.

The last witness was Patrolman Paschal. At first, he denied he had ever talked to King. In later questioning, however, he told the Judge that Mud Pitts, a longtime friend, had told him King wanted to see him.

"I told . . . (Pitts) I would meet him (King) up by what we call River Springs," Paschal said. "He (King) just more or less asked me if I would like to get a promotion on my job, that there had been some boys that know me who drive a truck and we are all friends, and they were interested in helping me get a promotion, and if I was interested in it he would be glad to help," Paschal said.

"What else was said at this time?" Judge Miller asked.

"Well, I just don't recall every little thing that was said," Paschal answered him.

Paschal insisted he had never discussed the

Hoffa case with his wife. In fact, Paschal said he
did not mention to his wife the strange circumstances under which he was offered a promotion.

"Did it occur to you that he was trying to reach
you and influence you so that you would influence
your wife?" Judge Miller asked.

"Nothing was said about it," Patrolman Paschal
again insisted.

"Wasn't it funny to you that a complete stranger
would offer to help you get a promotion?"

"I didn't know," Paschal answered.

After excusing the witness, the Judge said, "I
thin he (Paschal) discussed it with his wife. I
don't think there is any question about it. I don't
think he is entitled to credibility on his statement. I think she has, on the facts shown on this
record, been tampered with as a member of the
jury, and I so find."

Judge Miller ordered that Mrs. Paschal be
excused, and also ordered the jurors and alternates
"locked up" for the remainder of the trial.

Walter Sheridan was already gathering evidence
that indicated some Detroit Teamsters were at-
tempting to contact another juror, a 70-year-old
retired railroad mail clerk named Gratin Field. A
wide-ranging investigation brought no proof that
Fields had actually been contacted, but the fact
that an attempt to reach him had been made
seemed beyond question.

Testimony in the case was completed on December 20. If Fields was to be removed, it had to be
done immediately. Relying on Judge Miller not
to reveal important evidence, Prosecutor Neal
asked the jurist for a secret session.

"We hand to the court the Government's motion to strike Juror Number 12," Neal stated. Copies of bulky documents were handed to Judge Miller and Hoffa's lawyers. Then Neal added: "We have submitted to the court certain other documentary evidence enclosed in a sealed envelope, which because of the confidential nature of its contents, the Government requests . . . be sealed after the court reads and considers it."

Judge Miller read the secret papers and immediately ordered the clerk to reseal them: "It is very evident . . . from reading the sealed documents why they should not be released. It is also very evident from the content of the documents. . . that there is every reason for this court to believe that an effort has been made, if not actually accomplished, to influence this jury improperly. It is an astounding situation."

Defense lawyer Maher objected to dismissal of Fields. "There is nothing to even suggest a contact of a juror," Maher said.

"I am frankly astonished at the history of attemped jury fixing in this case," Judge Miller said in reply.

Defense lawyer James Haggerty complained that the sealed letter was "a pig in the poke," and contended that it placed the defense in "a ludicrous position."

Judge Miller said, "This is the most astonding, most amazing set of circumstances that I have ever seen . . . If an appellate court . . . should say that I have done wrong, that I have been in error in excusing these jurors, then they will just have to say it. I don't intend to sit here timidly and see efforts made almost before my very eyes to influence this jury improperly."

The Judge ordered dismissal of Juror Fields before instructing the jury. The jury's deliberations began at 3:02 p.m. on Friday. December 21. Four times, the jury reported that it was "hopelessly deadlocked," and on December 23, Judge Miller gave up and declared a mistrial. It was impossible to learn what influenced the decisions of individual jurors. The vote was 7 to 5 for acquittal.

Although the grueling nine-week trial yielded only an inconclusive hung jury, there were some rather conclusive comments by Judge Miller on the jury-tampering activities that had shocked his sense of ethics.

"I wish to make it very clear that I have no reason to doubt the honesty and integrity of any person called for jury service in this case," Judge Miller said.

Improper contacts were made

Then he gave the first public explanation of the mysterious secret sessions: "At these sessions, evidence was presented to the court indicating illegal and improper attempts were being made by close labor-union associates of the defendant (Hoffa) to contact and influence certain members of the jury.

"From the very outset while the jury was being selected . . ., there were indications that improper contacts had been made and were being made with prospective members of the jury," Judge Miller said and expressed his view that strong action was needed "to protect the court as and institution of government.

"The right of a defendant in a criminal case to be tried by a jury of his peers is one of the most sacred of our constitutional guarantees," the Judge declared. But, he went on to say, "the system of trial by jury . . . becomes nothing more than a mockery if unscrupulous persons are allowed to subvert it by improper and unlawful means.

"I do not intend that such shameful acts to corrupt our jury system shall go unnoticed by this court," Judge Miller said in quiet fury.

The Judge ordered a Federal grand jury convened to investigate the jury tampering and directed U. S. Attorney Kenneth Harwell to conduct other investigations as needed.

Nashville Teamster boss King was among the Teamsters and Teamster lawyers who flocked around Hoffa to offer congratulations after the trial. Hoffa's supporters regarded the hung jury as a victory, but their enthusiasm was cooled when Judge Miller ordered the broadest possible investigation of tampering.

Obstructing justice and jury tampering are felonies. Conviction on either charge can bring a prison term of up to five years.

LOOK MAGAZINE, MAY 19, 1964

A startling story of a murder plan and its aftermath, based largely on court testimony

BY CLARK R. MOLLENHOFF LOOK WASHINGTON BUREAU

Teamster Boss Edward Grady Partin startled the warden at the jail in the East Baton Rouge Parish Building on the morning of September 29, 1962, when he started to reveal a plot to assassinate Attorney General Robert F. Kennedy.

"This is something for the District Attorney's office to handle," said the warden, Capt. Thomas T. Edwards. "I don't want to know any more about it."

Edwards called the home number of William H.

(Billy) Daniels, an assistant to District Attorney Sargent Pitcher. Within an hour, Daniels arrived at the courthouse and took the elevator to the fourth-floor jail, where Partin was being held on a kidnapping charge that had grown out of a friend's domestic squabble. As the conversation started, Captain Edwards excused himself, explaining that "it isn't my business."

Alone with Daniels, Partin poured out the story. A few weeks earlier, when he had been in Washington at the International Teamsters headquarters, Partin said he was called into a Teamster office, and was asked about obtaining plastic explosives for the assassination of the Attorney General. "Something has to be done about that little s.o.b., Bobby Kennedy," Partin quoted a Teamster official as saying. "He'll be an easy target, always driving around Washington in that convertible with that big black dog. All we need is some plastic explosives tossed in with him, and that will finish him off."

Partin said he was told that some thought was also being given to using the plastic explosives on the Kennedy home at McLean, Va.

Partin, a Baton Rouge Teamster official, said he assumed he was approached because those involved in the assassination plot believed he was in so much trouble over a Federal criminal indictment that he would find the plan acceptable. He explained that some of the top Teamsters also knew he was a gun fancier, with a private gun collection, and might have convenient access to sources for explosives. Partin said he was asked to help in obtaining the plastic explosives far enough away from

Washington so they could not be traced back later
to those who would use them.

Daniels doubted the story of the assassination
plot, despite Partin's insistence that it was true.

Daniels knew that the Justice Department was
engaged in a comprehensive investigation of top
Teamsters officials in every part of the country.
Only three months earlier, a special Justice Department investigation-prosecution team headed
by Walter Sheridan, a special assistant to Attorney General Kennedy, had helped push through
the indictment of Partin on a 26-count charge involving alleged embezzlement of union funds and the
making of false entries in the books of Baton Rouge
Teamster Local 5. The indictment of Edward Partin was only a small part of the entire Teamster
bundle that at that time included 50 Teamster-
connected convictions.

Partin explained to Daniels that he had been concerned about the operations of the International
Teamsters Union for some time. He was irritated
with the lack of local autonomy under International
Teamster President James R. Hoffa, and he felt
that the power of the local officers and the union
members was being transferred to the top Executive Board and to Hoffa himself.

Ed Partin had been in the Teamsters Union for
12 years, and he was not inclined to be critical of
the rougher elements in the top ranks of the
1,600,000-member union. Many of them had been
jailed on charges ranging from burglary through
aggravated assault. It was easy for him to excuse
such records as a normal result of active work in
a tough union. Partin himself had been convicted

of burglary when he was 19, had engaged in fist fights and picket-line scuffles, and in 1962 stood accused by the Federal Government of loose use of union funds.

In his 12 years as business manager and secretary-treasurer of Local 5, Partin had become accustomed to some loose handling of union books, and condoning a bit of minor violence when necessary to make a point in a union-management dispute. But the idea of assassinating anyone — and particularly the Attorney General of the United States — was too much for him.

A plastic bomb plant at the Kennedy home would also endanger the Kennedy children, and Partin has small children of his own.

He had hidden his shock when the plot was mentioned, but he told Daniels that he had tried to contact Attorney General Kennedy and another top official. He had been brushed off by subordinates. He emphasized that he didn't want to tell his story unless it was to go to the top people. He didn't want to take a chance that word might leak out of the Justice Department to the International Teamsters Headquarters. He didn't want to jeopardize his job as a Teamsters official or his safety by being tabbed a "squealer."

Daniels told Partin that he thought he could arrange a talk with top Justice Department people, but that it would be necessary to discuss this with Pitcher first.

That evening Daniels and Pitcher returned to the East Baton Rouge Parish Building. Partin again told the story of the plot. Pitcher called New Orleans and reached Assistant United States Attorney

Peter Duffy. Duffy was told only that Partin wanted to talk to someone from the Justice Department about a "grave matter involving national security."

Duffy called A. Frank Grimsley, a Justice Department lawyer from Atlanta, who had been working with the United States Attorney's office on several Teamsters matters, including the investigation that had resulted in indictment of Partin a few months earlier. Partin's name and background were familiar to him.

Grimsley called Walter Sheridan, Robert Kennedy's special assistant, and Sheridan told him to leave for Baton Rouge as quickly as possible.

Sheridan treated the matter as routine. He knew of Ed Partin as a close friend of Teamster boss Hoffa and many other top officials in the International Headquarters and in the Southern Conference of Teamsters. Sheridan's unit had already been able to cultivate a half dozen informants among the men trusted by Hoffa and the Teamsters Executive Board, and another informant could always be helpful.

Sheridan's strongest interest at that time was in the trial of Hoffa scheduled to start before a Federal court jury in Nashville, Tenn., on October 22, 1962. Hoffa and another Teamster official were charged with having obtained $242,000 from a Detroit trucking firm in violation of the Taft-Hartley Act. The indictment charged that the money was paid through a truck-leasing firm partly owned in Mrs. Hoffa's name.

On Monday, October 1, at the FBI office in the Baton Rouge Post Office Building, Pitcher and

Daniels outlined the assassination plot to Grimsley and Assistant U.S. Attorney Duffy. Daniels explained that it would be best not to talk to Partin during the day. Too many people might note that Partin was talking with Federal officials.

It was after 2 a.m., on October 2, when Grimsley and Duffy returned to the East Baton Rouge Parish Building. At 3 a.m., Partin was brought from the jail to the District Attorney's office. From 3 a.m. until 6 a.m., he talked and answered questions for Grimsley, Duffy and Daniels. They reviewed the details over and over, and cross-examined the Louisiana teamster about the assassination plot and about many other matters. He cooperated fully.

Grimsley called Sheridan with full details of the alleged assassination plot. "Do you believe him?" Sheridan asked.

Grimsley said he was first inclined to discount the story as "too incredible" for belief, but that the cross-examination of Partin had convinced him that Partin was telling the truth. Partin had volunteered to take a lie-detector test, he said.

Sheridan was still skeptical. However, there were some routine things that had to be done. He notified Assistant Attorney General Herbert J. (Jack) Miller, head of the criminal division, Attorney General Kennedy and the FBI. Some basic security measures were urged with regard to the Attorney General and his family, including temporary abandonment of the convertible Robert Kennedy often used. The FBI was to arrange for a lie-detector test for Partin. If this indicated that Partin was truthful, then a number of additional security measures would be taken.

In five years of investigating corruption and racketeering in the Teamsters Union, Sheridan had learned not to be overly trustful of informants. He knew of Teamster efforts to plant double agents with the McClellan labor rackets investigating committee and even with the Justice Department.

Also, there were other matters of more pressing concern to him in that first week of October, 1962. The Federal court in Nashville had released the list of 35 names of the petit jury panel from which the Hoffa jury would be selected. From long experience, Sheridan was concerned about the possibility of jury tampering. In the "hoodlum empire" that surrounded Jimmy Hoffa, there were many men who might try to fix a jury if they felt they could get away with it.

The FBI report on the lie-detector test confirmed Grimsley's view that Partin was telling the truth. There was still no indication that Partin would be helpful in the major problem then at hand — the trial of Hoffa in Nashville.

On October 8, Partin called Hoffa in Washington to tell him he was out "on the street again." (Partin had been released on bail. The charge of kidnapping was later dropped.) Hoffa joked about Partin's jail time and warned him to be careful. Partin recorded the conversation with a device given to him by Daniels.

There were several more calls to Hoffa, and on October 18, Partin reached Hoffa at a Newark, N.J., number to complete arrangements to see the Teamster president about some union business.

"I will be in Nashville the weekend before the

twenty-second (of October)," Hoffa said. "Just come down to Nashville." Again Partin recorded the conversation.

On October 20, Partin called Grimsley in Atlanta, told him he was going to Nashville, and asked if there was anything the Justice Department wanted him to do.

"Just keep your eyes and ears open for any evidence of jury fixing," Grimsley said. He gave Partin the unlisted telephone numbers for Walter Sheridan's office in Nashville, and instructed him to call Sheridan on a pay phone when he had anything to report.

On the afternoon of October 22, Partin arrived in Nashville and checked in at the Andrew Jackson Hotel — temporary Teamster headquarters during the trial. While in the coffee shop waiting for Hoffa, Partin talked with Chicago insurance man Allen Dorfman, one of Hoffa's associates, and a dark-faced man he could not readily identify.

Partin and Sheridan's first meeting was in a room at the Noel Hotel. Partin told Sheridan that the dark man with Dorfman was Nicholas J. Tweel, a Huntington, W. Va., businessman. He reported that Tweel said Dorfman had asked him to "come down to Nashville and help him set up a method to get to the jury." (During the trial, Tweel and Dorfman both denied knowledge of any jury-fixing efforts.) Partin said that Hoffa himself had identified Tweel as a friend of Allen Dorfman who was "up here to help me."

Partin said that Hoffa had called him into his hotel bedroom and told him "to stick around a day or two" — that Hoffa might have one or two people for Partin to call.

"He (Hoffa) said that they were going to get one juror or try to get to a few scattered jurors and take their chances," Partin told Sheridan.

Partin said he met Ewing King, president of a Nashville Teamster local, and King told him "they had a meeting set up on the jury that night." On Tuesday, October 23, Partin left Nashville on union business, but relayed more information to Sheridan. Hoffa had "called me into his room and told me when I came back he may want me to pass something for him."

"He (Hoffa) put his hand behind his pocket like that and hit his rear pocket," Partin told Sheridan.

The jury was still being selected on October 23, when Federal Judge William E. Miller received the first firm evidence of jury tampering. James C. Tippens, a prospective juror, entered Judge Miller's chambers before 9 a.m. to tell the Judge that he had been offered a $10,000 bribe to vote for acquittal of Hoffa. The Nashville insurance man said that he was approached the afternoon of October 23 after court recessed. A neighbor had told him of the offer of "easy money."

Judge Miller thanked Tippens for reporting the incident, then called Government lawyers and Hoffa and his lawyers to his chambers and told them what had happened. He carefully avoided any charge that Hoffa or Hoffa's lawyers had a part in the bribe offer, but indicated shock and great concern.

Chief Prosecutor James Neal commented that there had been a number of illegal and improper telephone calls to jurors and added, "I am inclined to suggest at this point that the jury be locked up." Z. T. (Tommy) Osborn, Jr., one of Hoffa's lawyers, objected. He said the calls were probably the work of "crackpots and do-gooders."

Prosecutor Charles Shaffer said he had "no way of relating this to defendant Hoffa, but . . . the Government does know, and it is a public record, that jurors have been approached before (in cases) in which he is on trial."

There was a bombastic protest by defense lawyer William E. Bufalino who said Shaffer was merely passing on the unsupported allegations of Attorney General Kennedy.

Judge Miller did not want to lock up the jury for a six- or eight-week trial if it could be avoided. He felt disclosure of the attempt to bribe Tippens could serve as a stiff warning.

Partin returned to Nashville the next day, unaware of the Tippens incident. He reminded Hoffa that he had wanted him to "pass something" when he returned.

Hoffa, furious over Tippen's report to Judge Miller, told Partin, "The dirty bastard went in and told the judge that his neighbor offered him $10,000. We are going to have to lay low for a few days."

Partin called Sheridan the evening of October 25 to pass on the conversation with Hoffa, and the next day he called again to relate a conversation with Nashville Teamster boss King. Partin said King was making efforts to contact a woman juror whose husband was a highway patrolman. King was going to contact the highway patrolman, and "King also said he knew some lady who was a good friend of Mrs. Paschal and that he was going to try to have the lady sway Mrs. Paschal toward Hoffa."

Sheridan knew that Mrs. Betty Paschal, a pretty 35-year-old brunette juror, was the wife of Tennessee Highway Patrolman James Paschal of Woodbury, Tenn. Partin said that King had told him he was going to a place where the highway patrolmen "hang out" and talk to one of Paschal's closest friends.

Partin later told Sheridan of a conversation with King outside the court room in which King had pointed out a heavy-set dark-haired lady.

"King said that the lady was the one that came up to see if she could go home with Mrs. Paschal and talk to her," Partin told Sheridan. "After court recessed King (said) the lady had gone home with Mrs. Paschal."

That evening at Hoffa's hotel suite, Hoffa was upset over the testimony of a banker he felt had hurt him. "Hoffa then said he would pay $15,000 or $20,000, whatever it cost to get to the jury," Partin later informed Sheridan.

Partin left Nashville on October 31 for four days, but Sheridan had the FBI agents busy trying to corroborate Partin's reports. Sheridan didn't tell Prosecutors Neal and Shaffer of the information he was receiving, for there was no point in taking their minds off the trial.

On November 4, Partin returned, and the next day he phoned Sheridan. He quoted an irate Hoffa as complaining, "King keeps telling me he can get the patrolman but he don't get to him. He keeps talking about it and fumbling around."

King told Partin he believed Paschal would try

to influence his wife, and that King was supposed to meet the patrolman the following Sunday at a spring back of a farm near Woodbury, Tenn.

The next trial day was a bad day for Hoffa, and Partin said so to the Teamster boss. Partin said Hoffa quipped, "Well, don't worry about it too much. Because I have got the colored male juror in my hip pocket. One of my business agents, Campbell, came into Nashville prior to the trial and took care of it."

Partin said Hoffa told him that Teamsters Business Agent Larry Campbell "was kin to the (Negro) juror who wouldn't take any money but he wouldn't go against his own people." Hoffa said it looked like his best bet was a hung jury, and added, "If they have a hung jury, it will be the same as acquittal because they will never try the case again."

In leaving Nashville on November 7, Partin called Sheridan to say that King was complaining. Hoffa was "on King" for not making contact with Paschal and commenting that he wanted Mrs. Paschal influenced "for insurance," Partin said.

The FBI had started to work cautiously to determine the background and the travels of Larry Campbell, the business agent for Hoffa's Detroit Teamsters Local 299. Campbell was from Nashville, and still had relatives there, but he was not related to the one colored male juror, Gratin Fields. Campbell had an uncle, Thomas Ewing Parks, who worked in Nashville and who had had some contact with the family of Gratin Fields.

The FBI investigation had to be sharply restricted. The jury was not locked up. Fields and

Mrs. Paschal were going home each night, and it would be improper for the FBI to question relatives about the matter, for the questioning could be considered an "improper pressure" on the jurors if they learned about it.

Partin was back in the city on November 14 and 15, and reported to Sheridan that Hoffa was now "cursing and calling King a stupid s.o.b. for thumbing around and not getting the job (of contacting Paschal) done." On Saturday night, November 17, FBI agents trailed King as he drove to a restaurant on the edge of Nashville, swapped cars with George Broda, another Teamster official, and drove off in Broda's blue 1959 Ford in the direction of Woodbury, where the Paschals lived.

The car swap momentarily threw the FBI off the trail.

At 1:07 a.m. on November 18 another team of FBI agents noticed Broda's Ford parked at the Paschal home. Paschal, dressed in his highway patrol uniform, was standing in the drizzling rain talking to the driver of the car. Oscar (Mutt) Pitts, a friend of Paschal, had driven the 1959 Ford over to make arrangements for Paschal to meet with King at about 1:30 a.m. at a point called River Spring.

Other FBI agents noted the time Pashcal's car returned to the driveway in Woodbury, and still another FBI team trailed King back to Nashville. This was the first solid corroboration of the many reports that Partin had been making to Sheridan. Sheridan was elated, but there was still much work to do.

Hoffa, suspicious that someone was talking to

Sheridan, hired six off-duty Nashville police to tighten security, then picked Partin for the most sensitive job — guarding the door of Hoffa's suite.

An order locking up the jury became necessary on December 5, when a bloody altercation took place while the jury was out. A young mental patient had walked into the courtroom and fired a pellet gun at Hoffa. The pellet did not injure Hoffa, but free swinging fists and gun butts that felled the intruder created momentary chaos in the court.

If the jury had been present, it would have been grounds for mistrial. If the jury members found out it had happened, it might be grounds for mistrial, and Judge Miller had no alternative. The incident was a bit of good fortune for Sheridan, for with court permission, he was now able to broaden the inquiry into the report that Hoffa had tried to contact juror Gratin Fields and was trying to make contact with Mrs. Paschal. It was also possible to make more direct inquiry about the alleged effort to bribe Tippens.

On December 6, Neal and Shaffer asked for a secret hearing on King's effort to contact juror Paschal. Testimony of FBI agents was taken about the mysterious midnight rendezvous, and U. S. Marshal Elmer Disspayne was instructed to bring King and Paschal to the court. King entered the court, took a look at Hoffa and took the Fifth Amendment. Prosecutor Shaffer insisted Hoffa had flashed King a five-finger sign to take the Fifth Amendment. Hoffa insisted he was just rubbing his face.

Initially Patrolman Paschal denied that he had

talked with King, but later he told the Judge that Mutt Pitts had told him King wanted to see him up by River Springs.

"He (King) just more or less asked me if I would like to get a promotion on my job." Paschal insisted. He denied that King tried to discuss the Hoffa case. He insisted he had never mentioned to his wife the strange circumstances of the offer of a promotion. Judge Miller ordered Mrs. Paschal excused from the jury on the basis of reasonable evidence that an effort had been made to improperly influence her decision.

Sheridan and the FBI now concentrated on trying to corroborate the story Partin had told about Larry Campbell trying to make contact with Gratin Fields. Justice Department lawyers and a Detroit FBI agent went to work on the long-distance telephone calls and travel records out of Detroit to Louisville and Nashville. In Louisville, Paul Allred and FBI agents used an IBM machine on an around-the-clock schedule to sort more than 100,000 long-distance calls from public pay booths.

The week of December 16, when the Hoffa trial was drawing to a close, the results of telephone toll call studies appeared to corrobrate the Partin story. Larry Campbell had made contacts in Louisville with his uncle, Thomas Ewing Parks, and Parks in turn had reached persons in Nashville who had contacted a son and a daughter of Gratin Fields. It was strong circumstantial evidence, but it was still not enough to ask for removal of Gratin Fields from the jury panel. It was possible that no actual contact was made with Fields, but Sheridan did not feel he could take a chance. Neither did Attorney General Kennedy.

On December 19, Sheridan asked Partin if he would be willing to make a affidavit affirming that Hoffa had said "I have the colored male juror in my hip pocket." Partin agreed. His identity was to be kept secret from everyone except Judge Miller and the prosecutors. The notary public called to witness the affidavit had no knowledge of the importance of the person he dealt with.

Prosecutors Neal and Shaffer knew that Sheridan had an important informant, relative to the Paschal case, but knew only his code name of "Andy." On the eve of the action to remove Fields, they examined the Partin affidavit and learned that Partin was the informant.

The next day Neal told the court: "We have submitted to the court certain . . . documentary evidence enclosed in a sealed envelope, which because of the confidential nature of its contents the Government requests . . . be sealed after the court reads and considers it."

Judge Miller read the Partin affidavit. "It is very evident . . . from reading the sealed documents why they should not be released," the Judge said. "It is also very evident from the contents of the documents . . . that there is every reason for this court to believe that an effort has been made . . . to influence this jury improperly," he added. "It is an astounding situation."

Juror Fields was excused over the objections of defense lawyers. The case was submitted to the jury the next day. On December 23, the jury was reported "hopelessly deadlocked." The vote was 7 to 5 for acquittal of Hoffa. However, Judge Miller ordered an immediate investigation of the jury tampering charge. He said his order was not intended to reflect on any of those called for jury service in the Nashville trial.

Hoffa won the "hung jury" he wanted on the charge of violating the Taft-Hartley Act — and indictable misdemeanor with a maximum one-year prison term — but he was now under investigation for alleged jury tampering — a felony charge with a maximum five-year prison term.

Partin made one cautious visit to the Justice Department. John Cassidy, Sheridan's assistant, drove to Dulles Airport before 6 a.m. to escort Partin to Sheridan's unmarked office, where they discussed the personal risk Partin was taking in being a witness against Hoffa.

Partin was called as a witness before the Nashville grand jury in April, 1963, but Hoffa was unconcerned. Partin took the Fifth Amendment in line with instructions he received from Teamster headquarters. Not even the grand jurors knew Partin was a Government informant.

On May 9, 1963, the Nashville grand jury indicted Hoffa and six others on a charge of conspiracy to obstruct the administration of justice by jury tampering. There had been evidence against some of the defendants, but the case against Hoffa seemed largely circumstantial. Hoffa's lawyers believed their client was adequately insulated against direct implication.

The trial, which was transferred to Chattanooga, Tenn., started on January 20, 1964. For the first two weeks, Hoffa was his usual cocky self, and his attorneys were highly optimistic. Then at 1:50

p.m. on February 4, Ed Partin, who had been hidden on the outskirts of Chattanooga for three days, stepped through the rear door of the courtroom as the Federal Government's key witness.

Hoffa glowered with rage. Partin was one of the last Teamsters he expected to talk. Within a few minutes after Partin was given the oath, his testimony had implicated Hoffa, King and Larry Campbell with knowledge of the jury tampering in Nashville. Parks was the only defendent whose name was not brought into the testimony by Partin. With Hoffa prodding them, the nine defense attorneys made a frantic effort to suppress Partin's testimony.

Presiding Federal Judge Frank W. Wilson overruled their motion to bar testimony from Partin, and Special Prosecutor John J. Hooker brought out Partin's full story of his talks with Hoffa and others and the passing of information to Sheridan.

Two of Gratin Field's children — Carl Fields and Mrs. Mattie Leath — testified about the $10,000 bribe offer from Parks to Carl. Carl Fields admitted accepting $100 cash, but said there was no contact with his father. He said he lied to the FBI when first contacted, and that he had signed a false affidavit in the office of one of Hoffa's attorneys in Nashville.

Patrolman Paschal and Mutt Pitts testified that King tried to get Paschal to influence his wife to acquit Hoffa by promising him a promotion in the Highway Patrol. "I am sincerely sorry I furnished false information to Judge Miller and the FBI agents on December 6 . . . I had heard they (the Teamsters) were a rough bunch, and I thought I might wind up floating in a river with a log chain tied around me if I told anyone about this contact," he said.

The prosecuting attorneys avoided questioning Partin about the assassination plot conversations. Hooker and Neal said that the details of the assassination plot were immaterial.

The prosecution efforts to avoid the first conversations between Partin and Grimsley only made the defense lawyers more eager to explore them.

Prosecutor Neal objected to their attempts. In closed session, he warned, "This man (Partin) reported a threat by James R. Hoffa to kill the Attorney General."

"We have no objection (to the testimony)." attorney Harry Berke said for Hoffa. "We think it is so fantastic and unbelievable we are not trying to suppress it."

Judge Wilson ruled the plot talk immaterial to the jury-fix trial, and not to be explored.

Later, Harvey Silets, lawyer for Dorfman, pressed Partin with questions, and Partin cautioned, "It concerned something that I've been instructed not to say."

"Now in your course of meeting with (Daniels) . . . Mr. Hoffa's name came up?" Silets asked.

"In a manner not related to this (case), sir," Partin replied.

Grimsley, Daniels and Pitcher were all called to testify, as defense lawyers sought evidence inconsistency or grounds for mistrial.

Grimsley insisted the first calls from Assistant United States Attorney Duffy sketchily mentioned a "security" matter.

"Wasn't the name Hoffa mentioned at all?" Silets asked.

"No, I don't believe the name Hoffa itself was mentioned," Grimsley replied.

Grimsley said he was given details on the plot just prior to his meeting with Partin.

Judge Wilson then commented: "I will allow him to tell the subject matter of it, but it would not be appropriate to go into the details of it, gentlemen."

"Mr. Partin stated that in a conference with Mr. Hoffa —," Grimsley started, but was cut off by Judge Wilson, who said, "don't go into the details of it."

"Well, Mr. Partin stated that Mr. Hoffa told him that he would like —"

Again the Judge cautioned him against going into the details.

"An assassination plot," Grimsley testified.

"What is the date of that?" Silets asked him.

"That would be September or October, 1962," Grimsley said, believing that Silets had reference to his October 2 meeting with Partin.

"I'm inquiring about this conversation, reputed, alleged conversation between Hoffa and Partin," Silets corrected. "When was that to have taken place?"

"Sometime in the summer of 1962," Grimsley replied.

"Well, did you ever check it (the Partin story) out?" Silets asked.

"Yes, someone did," Grimsley answered.

"And what did you discover?" Silets asked.

"He (Partin) stayed somewhere in Washington,"

Grimsley replied.

"Did you discover whether he had seen the defendant, Hoffa?" Silets then asked.

"That I'm not certain of," Grimsley replied.

"As a matter of fact, he never did see the defendant, Hoffa, isn't that true? . . . Specifically in the summer of 1962, all your report discloses was that he was in Washington. You have no specific information of his being with the defendant Hoffa, isn't that right?" Silets pressed.

"I wouldn't know," Grimsley told him. "I haven't read the report lately."

Silets tried to characterize the assassination plot story as a "contrived circumstance" and "unsubstantiated wild charges" to hide improper schemes of wiretapping involving the Justice Department.

On cross-examination, Prosecutor Neal tried to refute comments by Silets tending to discredit Partin on the assassination plot story.

"Mr. Silets talked about a wild rumor and so forth respective to an assassination," Neal started his question. "Did you or someone give Mr. Partin a lie-detector test on that?"

"The FBI gave him one, yes," Grimsley replied.

"And what were the results?" Neal asked.

"That he was telling the truth," Grimsley replied.

Daniels was grilled by Silets.

"He (Partin) indicated to me that he had sought to make contact with a law-enforcement agency that he could trust in order to divulge what he termed a plot," Daniels explained.

Daniels said that in the investigation the Baton

Rouge District Attorney's office had recorded some of Partin's conversations with Hoffa in October, 1962. Daniels said that one recorded conversation "had its origin in a newspaper story that had appeared locally, either in the latter part of September or the first part of October, with the theft of a plastic explosive in the New Orleans area."

"Mr. Partin placed a call to Mr. Hoffa to apprise him of the fact that he had access to a supply of this plastic, as he termed it," Daniels testified.

"Did Hoffa actually speak to him, do you know?" Silets asked.

"This I don't remember, sir," Daniels replied.

"This conversation, did you hear Mr. Hoffa's voice on that recording?" Silets asked.

"I don't recollect that I heard Mr. Hoffa's voice on that recording," Daniels replied.

Grimsley was called back to the witness chair to clarify one point for the jury.

"Mr. Grimsley, you stated that one of the recordings had to do with an assassination plot," Prosecutor Hooker began.

"Yes, sir," Grimsley answered.

"Did it have anything to do with the assassination of President John F. Kennedy?" Hooker asked.

"No sir, it did not," Grimsley answered.

Sheridan, who was called by the defense, testified "instructions were given to the FBI to pursue the matter further . . ."

He testified he did not plant Partin in the Hoffa group, but added, "I was glad that he was there when he was there. In fact, he left many times when I wished he could have stayed there . . .

Each time I got information, it was turned over to the FBI. They conducted an investigation to corroborate the information, did corroborate it, at the time action was taken."

Hoffa was a snarling and argumentative witness under the cross-examination by stentorian-toned Prosecutor Hooker. Hoffa denied discussing jury fixing with Partin. He said he didn't know what King and other associates were doing.

The jury returned its verdict on March 4, finding Hoffa and three of the other defendants — King, Campbell and Parks — guilty of obstructing justice. The jury acquitted Dorfman and Tweel.

Judge Wilson sentenced Hoffa to eight years in the Federal prison and fined him $10,000. It was three-year prison terms for King, Campbell and Parks. All have appealed.

The full details of the assassination plot remained buried in FBI files, but the outline had emerged in the trial, as explanation of why Partin broke with the Teamster leadership. The 50-year-old Baton Rouge teamster had led a rough life, but experienced revulsion when it was suggested he obtain plastic explosives to assassinate Robert Kennedy. That evidence is still under active investigation by the FBI.

(The following material is reprinted from the Congressional Record, June 27, 1963. It was placed there by Senator Wayne Morse (D., Oregon) who identified it as captioned below.)

United States Department of Justice
PRESS RELEASE (undated)

"Summary of Past Criminal Actions Against James R. Hoffa"

In the past, the following criminal actions have been taken against James R. Hoffa, general president of the International Brotherhood of Teamsters:

1. On February 20, 1942, Hoffa and the late Owen "Bert" Brennan, a former vice president of the IBT, entered pleas of *nolo contendere* in Detroit, Mich., to Federal charges of violating the antitrust laws and were each fined $1,000.

2. Wiretap trials: On May 14, 1957, a Federal grand jury for the Southern District of New York charged James Riddle Hoffa, the late Owen "Bert" Brennan, and Bernard B. Spindel in a one-count indictment charging them with conspiracy to violate the wiretapping law. The indictment charged that beginning in 1953 the defendants conspired to intercept the telephone conversation of officials and employees of the Teamsters Union at the Teamsters headquarters, Detroit, Mich., who might be called to appear as witnesses before a congressional committee and a Detroit grand jury investigating labor racketeering. The first trial of this indictment resulted in a hung jury, and the

jury was dismissed on December 20, 1957. The newspapers reported that the jurors stood 11 to 1 for a conviction. Upon retrial the defendants were all acquitted on June 23, 1958.

3. Cheasty trial: On March 13, 1957, James R. Hoffa was arrested in the District of Columbia and charged with the bribery of John Cye Cheasty, an investigator for the McClellan committee. Mr. Hoffa was tried and acquitted during the summer of 1957 in the U. S. district court for the District of Columbia.

4. Sun Valley, Inc.: James R. Hoffa was indicted on December 7, 1960, in the Sun Valley matter on 12 counts of Federal mail and wire fraud. This indictment was dismissed on July 12, 1961, for defect in the selection of the grand jury. Mr. Hoffa was then reindicted on October 11, 1961, on 15 counts of mail and wire fraud and one of conspiracy. This matter is awaiting trial in the middle district of Florida.

5. Assault of Samuel Baron: On May 17, 1962, James R. Hoffa was charged with assault of Samuel Baron, a former IBT official, and released on $500 bail. On May 18, 1962, he pleaded not guilty to the above charge and demanded a jury trial. Baron subsequently withdrew the charges.

6. Test Fleet: On May 18, 1962, Hoffa was indicted in Nashville, Tenn., on charges of accepting payments from Commercial Carriers, Inc., between May 1949 and May 1958 in violation of the Taft-Hartley Act. On June 7, 1962, Hoffa entered a plea of not guilty. Trial started on October 22, 1962, and ended on December 23, 1962, at which time a mistrial was declared due to a hung jury.

LIFE

1180 CONNECTICUT AVENUE, N. W.
WASHINGTON 6, D. C.

EDITORIAL OFFICES
FEDERAL 7-8000

Thursday

Dear Ed:

I told Kennedy of your high interest and he is
delighted. He makes the suggestion that the piece go
into Baron's background and philosophy somewhat, to help
explain his disgust with Hoffa and his motivation for
breaking with the Teamsters. Kennedy believes deeply
that this is not a case of sour grapes, but of a man
acting out of conscience and principle. Kennedy thinks
the break will be understood better in light of his total
life in the labor movement.

Bob agrees that a ghost writer makes good sense,
and is agreeable to Graves and a writer you trust being
brought into the picture at this point.

Baron is out of town at the moment, but Kennedy thinks he'll be willing to return when I tell him
we want to proceed. I assume you'd like to crank this
up pretty quickly, so would you let me know who'll be
doing it and when you'd like Baron back here to go to
work. Since you'll only be talking about a writer and
a date, I see no reason you can't phone me on this point.

Best,

Hank

Hank Suydam

91

LIFE

Thursday

Dear Ed:

I told Kennedy of your high interest and he is delighted. He makes the suggestion that the piece go into Baron's background and philosophy somewhat, to help explain his disgust with Hoffa and his motivation for breaking with the Teamsters. Kennedy believes deeply that this is not a case of sour grapes, but of a man acting out of conscience and principle. Kennedy thinks the break will be understood better in light of his total life in the labor movement.

Bob agrees that a ghost writer makes good sense, and is agreeable to Graves and a writer you trust being brought into the picture at this point.

Baron is out of town at the moment, but Kennedy thinks he'll be willing to return when I tell him we want to proceed. I assume you'd like to crank this up pretty quickly, so would you let me know who'll be doing it and when you'd like Baron back here to go to work. Since you'll only be talking about a writer and a date, I see no reason you can't phone me on this point.

Best,
(Hank)
Hank Suydam

To____E. K. Thompson____

From___Suydam, Washington___ OFFICE MEMORANDUM

Date___March 6, 1961___

PERSONAL AND CONFIDENTIAL

Last Saturday I got a phone call from Bob Kennedy asking if I could
drop whatever I was doing and come to his office. I did, and when I got
there he closed the door and told me the following: in a back room was
a high official of the Teamsters, a man who had been privy to the inner
workings of the organization since 1953. He was particularly knowledgeable about Hoffa. This official is honest, said Kennedy, and also quite
an idealist. The man had been working directly with Kennedy and in
secret for the last two years. He was now so disillusioned and disgusted with the corruption he saw all around him, particularly as concerns
Hoffa, that he has just about decided to make a public break with the
union. Kennedy said he had suggested to this man that he make his break
via an article in LIFE in the form of a personal expose of Hoffa. Kennedy
asked my personal word that for the moment only you and I would know of
this matter. Kennedy feels, perhaps melodramatically, perhaps not, that
the man's life would be in danger if word leaked out of his intentions.
I told the Attorney General that if you were interested in this man's
story and if we did go ahead, more and more people at LIFE would have to
become involved. Kennedy understood this, but pointed out that if we
are not interested, then only two people, as he put it, that he personally
knows and trusts, will have had to know about it. I gave my word. He
also asked that if we do want to go ahead, or at least look into the
possibilities, in other words when we have to pass the point of only
you and I being involved, we let him know first. I said we would.

more...

To   E. K. Thompson
From   Suydam, Washington
Date   March 6, 1961

PERSONAL AND CONFIDENTIAL

Last Saturday I got a phone call from Bob Kennedy asking if I could drop whatever I was doing and come to his office. I did, and when I got there he closed the door and told me the following: in a back room was a high official of the Teamsters, a man who had been privy to the inner workings of the organization since 1953. He was particularly knowledgeable about Hoffa. This official is honest, said Kennedy, and also quite an idealist. The man had been working directly with Kennedy and in secret for the last two years. He was now so disillusioned and disgusted with the corruption he saw all around him, particularly as concerns Hoffa, that he has just about decided to make a public break with the union. Kennedy said he had suggested to this man that he make his break via an article in LIFE in the form of a personal expose of Hoffa. Kennedy asked my personal word that for the moment only you and I would know of this matter. Kennedy feels, perhaps melodramatically, perhaps not, that the man's life would be in danger if word leaked out of his intentions. I told the Attorney General that if you were interested in this man's story, and if we did go ahead, more and more people at LIFE would have to become involved. Kennedy understood this, but pointed out that if we are not interested, then only two people, as he put it, that he personally knows and trusts,

will have had to know about it. I gave my word. He
also asked that if we do want to go ahead, or at
least look into the possibilities, in other words
when we have to pass the point of only you and I
being involved, we let him know first. I said we
would.

At any rate, here's the story, as related to me
by this fellow after a cloak-and-dagger shift of
scenery, involving Kennedy slipping us out through
back corridors, a drive by roundabout route to the
guy's home in Virginia, and the assigning to me of
the code name "Brown."

Sam Baron is this gentleman's name. A small,
distinguished man of 58 with flowing white hair and
gray moustache, he has been deeply involved in the
labor movement or allied liberal causes since
1930. His present title is Field Director of the
Warehouse Division, a position in the executive
hierarchy just below the executive board. Baron
came into unionism through Dave Dubinsky's gar-
ment workers, and right away, he says, he encountered graft. Sam was in the investigative division, and he discovered that his own department
head was in collusion with New York gangsters.
The department head tried to discredit him with
the higher brass, but most of them were honest
and they backed his desire to prove what he suspected. Despite both threats and bribery attempts,
says Sam, he did, and his boss and a half-dozen
other department heads were fired.

In a couple of years Baron became involved with
the white collar organization drives in New York,
and 1935 saw him president of the Bookkeepers,
Stenographers and Accountants Union. It was at this

juncture that he encountered another in what he describes as a series of major challenges in his life. This one was communism. Baron was a socialist and very much opposed to the communists and especially their spreading influence in the labor movement. He has some stories about clashes he and the commies had which don't add anything to this summary, save to make the point, which Kennedy stressed to me, and which Baron quite modestly conveys, that he is both an idealist and a fighter for what he believes in.

At any rate, the Spanish civil war broke out, and in 1937 Sam went over in the dual role of reporter for several labor papers and as official observer for the Socialist party. He became a friend of Hemingway's, and together, says Baron, they witnessed the growing communist influence in the loyalist cause, and began to feel that many young Americans in Spain were being pathetically caught up in the clash between this communist influence on the one side and, of course, the Facists that the Americans had come to fight. More idealism, more soul-searching, brushes with the communists, including an attempt on his life, then, in 1939 out of Spain. Four years in New York where he tried his executive hand in a labor relations firm. He was finally hired in 1942 by the Textile Workers. His stint with them lasted until 1953, when Harold Gibbons, with whom he was developing a close friendship, asked him to come into the Teamsters. Baron accepted, and has been with them since.

"I've been in continuous association with and continuous clash with Jimmy Hoffa over since the day I went to work," says Sam. "One of the first things he ever said to me (perhaps he'd heard that I despised dishonest union officials) was: 'Don't think you're going to stop the boys from making a fast buck, because you're not!'"

Baron, who of course hasn't been the first one to do it, calls Hoffa "the most dangerous man in America." He says only someone like himself who has seen Hoffa operate from the inside can fully realize the "evil" of the man.

Says Baron: "Hoffa certainly has had as bad publicity as anyone around, but a lotta time it gets balanced off or rationalized with 'Well maybe he isn't the most ethical guy around, but he's done a lot for the rank and file Teamster,' or 'He's a pretty ruthless cookie, but personally he seems real nice. He doesn't smoke or drink, and he lives in a very modest house, and he's a devoted family man.' These people who say that would have been interested to see Hoffa the day after Victor Riesel was blinded. I think it happened around midnight in New York. Jimmy had an eight A.M. meeting with some of us in Chicago. Jimmy breezes into the room, makes straight for me and says gleefully, poking his finger in my chest: 'Hey Sam, a buddy of yours got it last night.' I asked him what he meant and he said: 'Your buddy, Victor Riesel, someone threw acid in his face. The son-of-a-bitch should have had it thrown on the hands he types with too.' Then Hoffa gave a big belly laugh. A few minutes later he got a call from O'Rourke in New York. Jimmy was saying to him, 'Boy, that's sure a shame about Riesel. I hope they get the bastard that did it.' When he hung up someone asked him since when had he developed all this

fast sympathy for Riesel, and Jimmy said, 'Don't
be stupid, you know that phone's tapped.'"

"Or some of his supporters should see the
pleasure Jimmy takes in trying to humiliate other
human beings to enhance his own ego. I was at a
conference in his office in Washington not long ago,
and one of the people present was Edward Bennett
Williams. Hoffa was flipping through some mail,
and all of a sudden, in front of everyone, he takes
one letter and, without looking up from his desk,
throws it on the floor. He said: 'Take care of that
Williams.' Some of these people in the organization are totally dependent on Hoffa, and have to
that that s____ from him, but Williams just got up,
didn't say a word, and just walked out of the room.

"Another time right in the middle of a big meeting, when I was disagreeing with him on a point,
Hoffa suddenly jumped up from the table. When he
gets really mad, he gets all red in the face, and
his eyes glare and you can see his facial muscles
working. 'Horsesh____!! he screams at me. 'What
the f____ do you know about anything. You're a f____-
ing square!'"

Baron says he's been able to live with his hate
of Hoffa because he believes strongly in the labor
movement and what he (Baron) can contribute. He
feels that the Teamsters Union particularly needs
honest officials, and he regards himself as that.
He says he believes that Gibbons, though more of
a "pragmatic operator" is honest and feels the
same.

He says the reason he thinks Hoffa has never
tried to get rid of him is twofold: Baron is Harold
Gibbons' boy and Hoffa badly needs Gibbons; Baron

is highly competent and also extremely popular with the rank and file, and Hoffa is acutely aware of this.

"Jimmy hates my guts. I don't know how many times he's stressed this in front of my colleagues. Time and time again he's said to me in front of them: 'Listen Baron. You depend on me for your job. I can take it anytime I want.'"

Of specifics regarding corruption, Baron says this: "I know of so much. My God, I'll bet Jimmy Hoffa has a couple of million dollars stashed away somewhere, but knowing about some of these things and proving them is another matter.

"Now for instance, I could write for you in detail the mechanics of how his election was rigged. It was rigged so tight what happened in Miami was no more an expression of the rank and file than I don't know what. I know how it was rigged — I saw it happen, but I can't prove it. Of course I don't think he had to rig it. If the rank and file had had a voice, I believe they'd have elected him. And I'm sure they will in this next election.

"I can talk about the intricacies of the Florida land business and the wiretap case.

"I'd like to reveal how he operates. Once in the early days of the labor rackets committee he called me in and closed the door. 'Baron,' he said, 'go downstairs to your office and burn all your records on such-and-such a matter and such-and-such a matter,' and I told him I had no reason to and had nothing to hid, and I locked up my records and refused." (Later, Baron turned over many things to Kennedy, including documents.)

"I can talk about the Cheasty bribery case. After

he got it set up, in what he thought was a foolproof way, he was going around bragging about having Cheasty 'on the committee and in my pocket.' That bribery was typical of a Hoffa operation. On anything that might cause trouble he works only in cash and there's no records of anything.

"The public should know that he tries to own anyone he can. Some columnists submit copy on him before it's published. I was right in the room when I saw Jim Bishop do it.

"I have talked at length to some of the wives of teamster officials, and they have some interesting things to say. Many are disturbed at what's happened during the last couple of years. Some have talked to their husbands often about the rightness or wrongness of what's going on in the union. Some accept and defend it, and others act as their husband's consciences. It's a fascinating interplay.

"I believe I could take your readers on quite a behind-the-scenes tour. Hoffa living in the very inexpensive home and driving the old car but right in his pocket most of the time is a roll of at least five thousand bucks.

"Hoffa the quiet family man contrasted with the ruthless image of him one night in the Woodner Hotel when he did such a job on Barney Baker because he didn't like his testimony before Bob Kennedy that he screamed and yelled at him like a madman and said things you don't say to another human being. Nobody in the Woodner nearby could sleep that night. Next day Baker had a heart attack.

"Well, I've had enough. Now the monitors are out, and Hoffa will be re-elected in June. His power is going to be absolute and if he ever acquires the domination over all transportation that he wants it will be an evil thing.

"You know, it's a terrible decision I face. I've pretty well decided to make this break. I'll be accused of selling out, of being a traitor and an informer. My family will suffer. But I really believe in the bottom of my heart that I will do the Teamsters and the labor movement more good than harm.

"I'm going to decide very shortly whether or not to make this break (another reason for Kennedy's caution — if, as is unlikely, Baron doesn't break, all this, of course, must never get out) but if I do, I'll tell you everything I know. I'll go the whole route on this story."

Are you interested in pursuing this further? A lot of what he says has been said in so many places before. The expose stuff sounds interesting, but to me at least, pretty undocumentable and therefore probably very libelous. But the more personal stuff on what Hoffa is like and how he behaves sounds pretty good. The basic situation of a fairly high Teamster official breaking publicly because of the corruption he's seen all around him is quite dramatic, and if he does it through us, it could be quite a piece. What he wants to do, if you show initial interest, is sit down and write something rough on his own. He's very verbose and my worry here would be that such a document might still not help you reach a final decision. You might prefer to have a collaborator go to work with him from the start. At any rate, he'd probably be agreeable to anything you suggest. Incidentally, I did not discuss money at all.

Of course this guy has an axe to grind and SO, as you of course know, does Bobby Kennedy (see the Kennedy-Hoffa cartoon in yesterday's News of the Week in Review section of the Times).

Anyway, that's the story. If you'd like to have Graves or one of the text writers go into this more deeply with Baron, still just on an exploratory basis, I'm sure Kennedy and Baron will buy that.

Incidentally, since I gave the assurance I wouldn't handle any of this by phone, except in the most general way, could you respond on paper? Please be sure the envelope is plainly marked P&C for while I trust BJ completely, I do want to keep my bargain with Kennedy, and her husband is in the Justice Department.

Best regards.

HENRY MAYER
19 West 44th Street
New York 36, N.Y.

December 10, 1962

Mr. James Haggerty, Vice-President
WABC
7 West 66th Street
New York 23, N.Y.

Dear Mr. Haggerty:

I protest against WABC's failure to edit the program "All America Wants To Know" which was televised on December 9, 1962 from 3:30 to 4:00 P.M.

Senator John McClellan, when interviewed by reporters about ten days ago regarding the implications of the current National Labor Relations Board contest between the Communications Workers of America and the Teamsters Union over the Western Electric Installers, took the fair and lawyer-like position that since a criminal trial involving charges against James Hoffa was going on in Tennessee, he would make no comment.

The judicious Senatorial toga was doffed completely, however, on WABC on Sunday and was replaced by a hatchet job on the part of the Senator, replete with the usual name calling and, beyond that, the extreme characterizations of Hoffa as "a menace to society", "a threat to our national safety and welfare", as well as the usual tripe about the Teamsters taking control of the nation through its power to tie up transportation, etc.

Coupled with the verbal brickbats was the visual display of McClellan's new book *Crime And Punishment*, with the implicit indication to the watchers that Hoffa should not go scot-free again — all with the obvious hope, that if Hoffa's "jury of his peers" were among the viewers (and they probably were) the "crime" this time would not go "without punishment".

This is the kind of shameful misuse of one of our important communications media, which in Great Britain would have sent all of the participants to jail for contempt of Court. It might very well result in a mistrial or a reversal of any finding of guilt in the present Hoffa trial.

Incidentally, the book of my colleagues in the American Civil Liberties Union, Edward Bennett Williams — *One Man's Freedom* — will remain part of our literature long after Senator McClellan's carefully selected rehash of his Committee's proceedings will molder into dust.

If the television network wishes to avoid censorship — and I think it should — then it will have to practice self-discipline — something which was wholly lacking when the tape of "All America Wants To Know" was allowed to pass unchanged.

Of course, if the Teamsters Union is to be considered fair game for the same reason that it is regarded as anathema by our Arkansas-oriented Senator, i.e. that it is a powerful union, then we might as well forget about all of our civil liberties, including those of Television.

> Sincerely yours,
> (Henry Mayer)
> HENRY MAYER

21. That on the 22nd day of July, 1959, the De-
fendant, Kennedy, appeared on The Jack Paar Show
at or about 11:15 P.M. over station WRCA-TV (NY)
(Channel 4) and The National Broadcasting Company
Television Network, and the Defendants, Kennedy
and Paar, intentionally, maliciously, carelessly,
wrecklessly and with malice aforethought, de-
famed the Plaintiff, James R. Hoffa, as stated in
Exhibit "A", attached hereto and made a part here-
of, in particular, but not limited to the statements
made as herein indicated by the Defendants:

(p. 3)
PAAR: ". . . tell us about Hoffa, as much as you
wish. You know the laws of libel."
KENNEDY: ------
(p. 4)
PAAR: "Forgive me for interrupting, but I think
it's important that you say what do the Teamsters include. I was amazed how broad a term
that is."
KENNEDY: "Well, it's really anything, anything
and everything. It's basically trucking . . .

"They can close down most of the metropolitan areas in the United States. And the fact that
it is controlled at the top — certainly the vast
majority of Teamster members and Teamster
officials are honest, but it's controlled and dom-
inated at the top by racketeers and gangsters,
and people who are not interested in union, or
interested in bettering the lives of their fellow-
man — which union officials should be and which

the vast majority are — but only interested in
stealing or extorting money, or betraying the
union membership.

* * *

PAAR: "Do you feel what you've just said, and
what you believe hurts your brother's chances?"
KENNEDY: "I don't think that he is — he feels the
same way. And I don't think that that should affect it one way or another. We both realize that
this is the — a major problem in the United
States. And unless something is done about it,
this country is not going to be controlled by
people such as yourself, or people such as are
here, but are going to be controlled by Johnny
Dioguardi and Jimmy Hoffa, and Tony Duch
Koralo and these people who are gangsters and
hoodlums.

* * *

(p. 5)
PAAR: "The question then is — Is Hoffa an im-
provement over Dave Beck?"
KENNEDY: "Oh, there's no comparison between
Mr. Hoffa and Mr. Beck. Mr. Beck is just a
thief . . . I think — this — this . . ."
PAAR: "We may be in court together, You and I
. . . I hope to hell you know what you're doing
. . . because I owe plenty. I'm just . . ."
(Long Applause)
KENNEDY: "Mr. Dave Beck. . ."
PAAR: "Joseph Welch watches this show every
night so maybe, I think . . ."
KENNEDY: "Mr. Beck has been convicted of steal-
ing money, so — from the union. I say that there
is no comparison. Mr. Hoffa is a far more seri-

ous threat than Mr. Dave Beck, and of course he's been in as many financial deals. He was set up in a trucking company by an employer after he set — came in and settled a strike against the employees. He's been — of course Mr. Beck at least had records: Mr. Hoffa deals only in cash. He deals with many employers. He has made side deals with some of the biggest companies in the United States. It is a — we can find nowhere . . ."

* * *

(p. 6)

KENNEDY: "Well, we've been in-exposed at least 50 big companies and corporations since the beginning of this committee, some of the biggest in the United States, who have been involved in various deals."

PAAR: "Big fine companies, well-known companies?

KENNEDY: "Would you like me to name some of them?"

PAAR: "I've never backed down yet."

KENNEDY: "Well, the Anheuser-Busch Company, the Fruehauf Trailer Company, the Association Transport Company all had deals with Dave Beck."

PAAR: "None of our sponsors. Go on. . ."

KENNEDY: "Sears Roebuck Company, Morton Frozen Food Company, the Whirlpool Company . . ."

PAAR: "You're getting warm" . . .

KENNEDY: ". . . with Nathan Shefferman. You have some of the biggest restaurants in the Chicago area who had set up and hired gangsters

and hoodlums for a period of some 20 years to
handle their Labor-Management relations. The
Commercial Carriers Company of Michigan,
which has a big trucking company, set Dave
Beck — set Jimmy Hoffa up in a trucking company after he came in and settled a strike for
them.

"You have the fact that Dave Beck — that
Jimmy Hoffa has had side deals with the Ries-
Riss Trucking Company, and other trucking companies, which is against the interests of the
union membership. . ."

*   *   *

(p. 7)

PAAR: "Have you ever spoken so frankly before —
the public?"

KENNEDY: "I don't think I've ever been asked
questions like this before. I have not."

*   *   *

KENNEDY: ". . . The contracts that are the lowest
contracts, which are for over-the-road drivers,
are in the Central Conference of Teamsters, and
those are contracts that he has negotiated. They
are lower than the contracts for the rest of the
Teamsters."

*   *   *

KENNEDY: ". . . At least 75 per cent of the dele-
gates that participated in the election of Mr.
Hoffa down in Miami, Florida, were elected il-
legally. And you can ask how that happened. It
happened by Mr. Dave Beck just waiving the
Constitution.

"If you tried to oppose the Teamsters, sup-
posing you were just an ordinary truck driver,

you would immediately lose your job; you can't
support your wife and your family; you would
have a very difficult time finding jobs in that
community. And we've had instance after instance of that. You certainly can't — you can't
run for office. They have provisions in the Constitution that — forbade — forbid or prevent
many of these people from running for office
even at the local level. You are absolutely pow-
erless."

* * *

(p. 11)

KENNEDY: "Oh, I think that they seem to feel, and
I think that if you watched the hearings you can
see that they feel that they are above the law
and the government of the United States — he and
his colleagues. There's no question about that.
They feel that — that nobody can touch them, that
they can fix juries, that they can fix judges, that
they can fix members of the legislature. They
don't have to worry about this. They have enough
money. They have — Mr. Hoffa has said in the
past, every man has his price. So they don't
worry; they're — they're not concerned about
that.

"They were doing things in 1958 and this year,
1959. Mr. Hoffa and his chief lieutenants were
involved in matters which were equally as bad
as what we developed in 1955 and 1956. They're
keeping up the same thing. I think that there are
many honest Teamster officials. They can't do
anything at the present time. I think if they get
some help from the courts, they get some help
from some of the Monitors, that their — Mr.

Hoffa can be removed and some of the honest officials, such as Jim Lukens from Cincinnati — there are many honest Teamster officials on the West Coast . . ."

PAAR: "Are there many who fight Hoffa within the . . ."

KENNEDY: "There are some; I don't think that there are very many. Many of them are waiting to have Mr. Hoffa removed, and then they will come forward. This is unfortunate, but it's true. But many of them are honest nevertheless."

PAAR: "Do you think it will happen?"

KENNEDY: "Yes, I do. I don't think there's any question. I — you just can't — this country can't survive if you have somebody like him operating. And this country's going to survive. He feels that he's bigger than the country, he and his lieutenants. And I don't think that that's true."

PAAR: "He seems to win all the battles, doesn't he?"

KENNEDY: "He won't win in the end."

PAAR: "Not the war, huh?"

KENNEDY: "He won't win in the end."

PAAR: "The battles, but not the war."

22. *That on the 26th day of July, 1959, the Defendant, Kennedy, appeared on "MEET THE PRESS" at or about 6 P.M. over Station WRCA-TV (NY) (Channel 4) and the National Broadcasting Company Television Network, and the Defendant, Kennedy pyramided his libels and slanders and defamed the plaintiff, James R. Hoffa, as stated in Exhibit "B" attached hereto and made a part hereof, in par-*

*ticular, but not limited to the statements made as
herein indicated by the Defendant, Kennedy:*
(p. 2)

SPIVAK: "Mr. Kennedy, the other night on The
Jack Paar Show you made some serious charges
against Mr. Hoffa outside of your investigation,
and he threatened to sue you for libel. Will you
tell us what your reaction is to that threat? Do
you think you can prove the charges you made
against him?"

KENNEDY: "Oh, I feel that in our investigation
that we have shown that Mr. Hoffa has made
collusive deals with employees, that he betrayed
the union membership, that he sold out the union
membership, that he put gangsters and racketeers in important positions of power within the
Teamsters Union, that he's misused union funds.
I say that, and I will say it again. If Mr. Hoffa —
If Mr. Hoffa will sue me, I think we can take
that to a court and allow it to be decided by a
jury. And I'm sure that Mr. Hoffa should feel
that if he loses that case, that he should resign
as International President of the Teamsters.
Because if he is guilty of any one of these things,
he's not worthy to be — to be International President of that union."

SPIVAK: "Mr. Kennedy, you charged Mr. Hoffa at
last hearing with a betrayal of his union membership, betrayal of his own membership. Have
you got any evidence to prove that? I thought
most of the Teamsters were fairly well sold on
the wages he's gotten for them the fringe benefits he's gotten for them, and everything else."

KENNEDY: "Well, Mr. Spivak, let's say this: that

the Teamsters contracts, as a general proposition, are high, with some major exceptions, but they are generally high; but the highest contracts have been negotiated in the eastern section of the United States with over-road truckers; but the contracts that Mr. Hoffa has negotiated in the Central Conference of Teamsters are not as good contracts; that, in addition to that, Mr. Hoffa has made collusive deals with employers, which, although the terms of the contract might read very well, that he has gone behind the terms of the contract and made secret deals with the employers."

(p. 4)

SPIVAK: "Well, Mr. Kennedy, are these statements that you made with the immunity of your committee, or are these things that you could prove in a court of law? There is a vast difference, and I think you will admit that."

KENNEDY: "No I think that — these are things that have been established as factual material before the committee, and these are the type of thing which I — I claim and feel, and the committee feels — has betrayed the union membership continuously. I say that Mr. Hoffa and those around him are not interested in the union membership; they are only interested only in themselves, only in bettering their own lot; that they have not helped or benefitted the union membership, that the best contracts are by honest union officials — Mr. Tom. . . Mr. Tom Hickey, up in New York, Local 807, the local in Pittsburgh, the locals in Ohio which have been run by Mr. Jim Lukin, some of the locals out in the Western

Conference of Teamsters. Those locals have the best contracts. They have nothing to do with Mr. James Hoffa."

BROOKS: "Mr. Folliard."

FOLLIARD: "Counsellor, a little while ago you watched Mr. Hoffa on the Face the Nation program. What did you think of his performance?"

KENNEDY: "Well, I think that it was most unfortunate, Mr. Folliard, that questions were not asked regarding his own activities and the activities of his chief lieutenant. I understand there was some agreement that was made with Mr. Hoffa that they would restrict the questioning to just legislation. I think this is most unfortunate. I don't think that you should — that the Attorney General — it would have been well for the Attorney General to debate the tax laws with Al Capone. And I don't think it's well for — to discuss legislation with Mr. James Hoffa.

"I think it's worthwhile if you have him on a program and ask him for explanations of the sellout of union members, for the misuse of union funds or any of these other things. But I don't think it's very interesting to find out what Mr. Hoffa thinks of legislation. He is the chief reason why legislation's being considered, he and his chief lieutenant."

*   *   *

(p. 5)

FOLLIARD: "Now what about the Board of Monitors appointed by a Federal Judge here to oversee the affairs of the Teamster's union. Would that Board of Monitors, by a vote of two to one, have the power to bring about Hoffa's ouster as president of the Teamsters union?"

KENNEDY: "They would have the power to take the first major step in that direction, to call for his ouster. And then there would have to be a trial, which I think would have to be supervised by either the court or by somebody appointed by the court. But they definitely have the power to move against Mr. Hoffa personally, and I would think that — that there is a very good chance that they will do so."

* * *

(p. 6)

MRS. CRAIG: "Has a libel suit been filed against you yet? Do you know what he's suing you for?"

KENNEDY: "I do not."

CRAIG: "What do you think he's suing you for. . ."

KENNEDY: "I don't know."

CRAIG: ". . . don't you know?"

(p. 7)

KENNEDY: "I don't know."

CRAIG: "There was one thing he said he'd sue you for, but you didn't mention that on the air, did you, the other night?"

KENNEDY: "I believe not. I don't — I don't — I do not know what he's suing me for. I haven't heard from him personally or from his attorney."

CRAIG: "You said you'd welcome the suit. Why do you welcome the suit?"

KENNEDY: "I'd welcome it because I think that it be well — Mr. Hoffa complains that they have no right of cross-examination, that the — that the hearings are not fair, I think that we — I made these charges about him, I feel them very strongly, and I think the record supports them. And I think that it would be well to submit that to a jury, and make its decision. But I think it should be understood that Mr. Hoffa, if he is not sustained in — in his charges that I've committed libel against him, should resign as international president."

CRAIG: "Your committee did not get much out of Mr. Hoffa, could the Courts get more?"

KENNEDY: "Mr. Hoffa would have to answer all the questions certainly before — in court. . ."

CRAIG: "You mean in a libel suit, you mean he would have to testify in a libel suit?"

KENNEDY: "That's correct."

CRAIG: "Under oath, and would be compelled to answer?"

KENNEDY: "That's correct."

(p. 11)

POLLIARD: "What is he hiding: What — why — are they afraid to answer questions with respect to Mr. Hoffa's affairs?"

KENNEDY: "Well, Mr. Hoffa holds their life and death as far as their jobs are concerned, many of them making thousands and thousands of dollars. For instance, his friend out in Chicago is receiving a salary equivalent — equivalent to $90,000 a year, and he doesn't want to give that up. And if he has some explanation for Mr. Hoffa, Mr. Hoffa assures him if he comes in and takes the Fifth Amendment, he'll maintain his position."

DWM

October 8 200